Our Highest Calling

Welcoming Others to Christ

through Discipleship

in Love

Sang W. Sur, Ph.D., Th.D.

© 2020 Sang Sur

Published by Prayer Tents Media
Old Tappan, NJ

All rights reserved. No portion of this book may be reproduced, stored in a retrieval system, or transmitted in any form or by any means—electronic, mechanical, photocopy, recording, scanning, or other—except brief quotations in critical reviews or articles, without the prior written permission of the publisher.

Scripture quotations are taken from the Holy Bible, New Living Translation, copyright © 1996, 2004, 2015 by Tyndale House Foundation. Used by permission of Tyndale House Publishers, a Division of Tyndale House Ministries, Carol Stream, Illinois 60188. All rights reserved.

ISBN 978-1-953167-00-2 (Hardcover, English)

ISBN 978-1-953167-07-1 (Softcover, English)

ISBN 978-1-953167-02-6 (Kindle e-book, English)

ISBN 978-1-953167-04-0 (Other e-book, English)

ISBN 978-1-953167-03-3 (Hardcover, Korean)

ISBN 978-1-953167-08-8 (Softcover, Korean)

ISBN 978-1-953167-09-5 (Other e-book, Korean)

Library of Congress Control Number: 2020942011

Advance Praises for *Our Highest Calling*

A great book to read! Dr. Sur did an excellent job, candidly pointing out the overlooked areas of evangelism and discipleship in relation to mission as he emphasizes how evangelism, mission and discipleship are inseparable. You will be challenged and convicted without condemnation and be inspired by the Holy Spirit as you rethink about the Love Commandment of Jesus Christ in conjunction to the Great Commission.

Dr. Sur's Highest Calling book will help young Christians with the biblical foundation and redirect seasoned Christian leaders to evaluate the unhealthy church tradition and culture in order to move upward to the highest calling!

Dr. SueLee Jin, Pastor, Mentor, and Friend of Sang

Dr. Sur beautifully illustrates and explains what discipleship is. He guides us through why we should focus on it and how to put it to practice and raise up new disciples through small groups. This book will be an insightful, practical, and helpful guidebook for small group leaders and for those who want to grow spiritually through serving others.

Paul Hyon, President, Korean CBMC of North America

I highly recommend Dr. Sur's book, Our Highest Calling, where he addresses the need for the preaching of the gospel through small groups. Strategies for presenting the gospel are shaken as contextualization becomes the emphasis in leading people to Jesus. Even in the midst of social unrest and an unprecedented pandemic, Christ's commission must be fulfilled. Pastors cannot fulfill the great commission alone. The tentmaker, business person, employee, and truthfully, all Christians can take the initiative to minister to others by leading a small group. Evangelism through love is a timeless concept which Dr. Sur handles deftly as he deals with the hurdles of the day. Jesus modeled ministry through his relationship with his disciples—the first small group sodality. Dr. Sur very adequately lays the groundwork for us to follow Jesus's lead.

Dr. Dwight Haymon, Pastor, Lifegate Church International

"Our Highest Calling: Welcoming Others to Christ through Discipleship in Love" is a scholarly and well-researched guide to fulfilling the Great Commission by making disciples in small groups.

Dr. Sur, herein, draws our attention to Ephesians 4:16, showing us how the whole Body of Christ becomes fitly joined together in love.

I strongly recommend this book, birthed in the author's heart, out of the personal experience, and a God-given burden to see the Great Commission fulfilled through true discipleship.

Dr. Bob Alarid, World Ablaze Ministries

Our Highest Calling

Make disciples of all nations as you are going, baptizing, and teaching.

Matthew 28:19-20

The Great Commission is a way of life. It is something to be carried out as one is going about. It is not a one-time evangelistic event. It is a call to make disciples as we live out our lives.

In our modern day, Christians have fallen prey to the trends of the world, including idolizing busyness and individualism, which are counter to the love that God called us to share and the community we are to be. The center of focus of the Early Church was love toward God and others, which fulfilled the Greatest Commandment.

Our Highest Calling is about how to live out that life, and it is through discipleship that we can make disciples in our lives. Discipleship is a practice of love with other close-knit Christian brothers and sisters over time. It is about being available for one another and pursuing God-given callings together for the kingdom of God. As Christians grow in discipleship and form deep relationships, they will in turn make disciples who truly love God. They can then walk together and make even more disciples, just as Jesus and His disciples did throughout their lives.

Dedication

Thank You, Jesus.

To my children:

    Samuel, may you be the leader of God's people, the one who hears from God, and a counselor to the mightiest kings.

    Esther, may you be the lover of God, the one who is compassionate, and an intercessor who brings many to the Lord.

To my wife:

    Jihyung, my life would never have been the same without you. Thank you for enabling me to go after the call of Jesus by supporting and encouraging me through it all, now for about half our lives. I love you. Let's finish the call of God together.

To all who are seeking God, whether today or sometime during your life, may you find Christ through the lives of Christians around you.

Acknowledgments

Thank you, CBMC brothers in New York City, New Jersey, and Long Island for teaching me true fellowship. Such love cannot be received from anywhere else.

Thank you to all my mentors along the way, including:

Pastor and lawyer Sam Hwang, who exemplified Christian leadership in the marketplace;

Dr. SueLee Jin, my mentor for Doctor of Ministry (D.Min.) who prayed for and encouraged me way beyond the degree; and

Dr. Tae Moon Park, my mentor for Doctor of Theology (Th.D.), who got me to dig deeper into theological aspects of discipleship.

Thank you to all my friends:

New Jersey and New York pastors who stand by and labor together with me for the gospel of Jesus.

Alex "Dong Ha" Kim, who seemingly invaded my privacy in many ways to teach me true brotherhood and friendship. I am forever indebted to you, my friend. See you in heaven.

Andrew Lee, my childhood friend, with whom I spent endless time loitering and doing nothing together in front of the yard at P.S. 199, for reminding me what it means to be there for each other, even when nothing seems to be happening.

And to all my friends who have shown me measureless love over the years.

Foreword

The apostle Paul told Timothy, *Thou therefore, my son, be strong in the grace that is in Christ Jesus. And the things that thou hast heard of me among many witnesses, the same commit thou* **to faithful men**, *who shall be able to teach others also* (2 Timothy 2:1–2 KJV, bold added). Dr. Sang Sur is such a faithful man. Our Highest Calling is visible evidence of the author's faithfulness in life and ministry.

The apostle Paul also shared his heart of ministry, telling the Thessalonian Christians that they had become very dear to him: *We loved you so much that we shared with you not only God's Good News but our own lives, too* (1 Thessalonians 2:8). *Our Highest Calling* is a compelling commentary on a love-based ministry that cries out for disciple-making in the Church.

Love must precede all things!

Over time, I have come to know Dr. Sur quite well and very closely. I clearly feel his heart for the kingdom of God, for the person and gospel of Jesus Christ, for the church of Christ, and even for the lost, just as he has verbally expressed to me on numerous occasions.

Dr. Sur presents an excellent case for small groups and provides a powerful and effective context and methodology for disciple-making when small groups are done right. Dr. Sur also makes a compelling case for *life-on-life* discipleship through careful exegesis of Scripture, the history of the church, and experiences of his own, as well as of others.

A clear understanding of the Great Commission of our Lord Jesus Christ is critical, and Dr. Sur provides an admirable exegesis of discipleship based on the Great Commission passage. Very few people today desire to be discipled, and even fewer people desire to disciple others. Therefore, Dr. Sur's challenge to us to *return to discipleship is timely.*

A serious lack of margin in life, particularly a lack of time in the life of both the moderns and post-moderns, poses a great threat to honoring our highest calling. Someone who is self-focused cannot love someone else. Someone who cannot make time for others does not love them.

Jesus Christ came to earth to spend time with sinners like me. He poured His love and, indeed, His life into godless sinners such as fishermen and tax collectors. The Great Commission is the call of Jesus Christ for His disciples to do likewise. This book takes you through the journey of why and how to love others.

Thank you for writing this book, Dr. Sur.

From Philadelphia,
Sam Y. Hwang

Contents

Preface. Bringing People to Christ 1

Chapter 1. The Great Commission 5
    Evangelism, Missions, and Discipleship of Jesus's Disciples 6
    The Call to Make Disciples 9
    The Meaning of Discipleship 11
        It Is the Collective Calling of All Believers, the Church of Jesus Christ 12
        It Is the Call to Go After Those Who Do Not Know God. 13
        We Are to Make Disciples as We Are Going, Baptizing, and Teaching. 15
        We Are to Guard Our Faith and Pass It Along. 21
        We Are to Trust God. 22
    The Great Commission and Jesus/Disciples Doing Discipleship 23

Chapter 2. The Good News Explained 27
    Discipleship Requires Relationships That Are Dependent on the Learner 35

Chapter 3. How Jesus and His Disciples Made Other Disciples 43
    How Jesus Did Discipleship 43
    How Jesus's Disciples Did Discipleship 46
    The Gospel and Intercession of Believers 49

Chapter 4. History of the Gospel, Evangelism, and Missions..53

The Great Commission as Shown in the Scriptures 54

The True Gospel Message That Jesus and His Disciples Taught 55

The Great Commission as Shown in the First Millennium 57

How the Gospel Was Understood until the Protestant Reformation 60

The Great Commission in the Second Millennium 63

State of the Great Commission Today 65

John Wesley's Method of Discipleship—Class Meetings 69

Chapter 5. Effective Strategies for Evangelism 75

Jesus's Call to Make Disciples 77

Passionate Prayer Meetings in Small Groups That Changed the World . 79

Small-Group Movement Outside the Modern-Church Structures - Modalities and Sodalities 86

Contextualization—Understanding People Where They Are and Speaking in a Way They Can Understand 90

Use of Business Models to Reach the Less Accessible 96

Theology of Contextualization 101

Interest-based Small Groups 107

Reliance on the Holy Spirit to Do Mighty Things through Small Groups 109

Chapter 6. Our Highest Calling Is Love 113

What Should a Small Group Look Like? 116

An Experiment to See What an Unchurched Person Seeking God Might Experience 117

2 Peter 1:5–9: Our Highest Calling Is Love 120

    Faith 123

    Moral Excellence 124

    Knowledge 125

    Self-Control 127

    Patience 128

    Godliness 129

    Love, Brotherly Love 132

    Love—Agape Love 135

The State of the Church Today 136

1 John 4:7–8: God Is Love 138

1 Corinthians 13: Love in Practice 140

    Love is patient. (v. 4) 143

    Love is kind. (v. 4) 144

    Love is not jealous, boastful, or proud. (v. 4) 146

    Love is not rude and does not demand its own way. (v. 5) 150

    Love is not irritable, and it keeps no record of being wronged. (v. 5)
    151

    Love does not rejoice about injustice, but rejoices whenever the truth wins out. (v. 6) 153

    Love never gives up or loses faith. Love is always hopeful and endures through every circumstance. (v. 7) 154

    God Is Love, and He Calls Us to Represent Him 155

Chapter 7. Being a Disciple to Make Disciples 159

    Basic Structure of a Small Group 160

        Foundational Structure 1: Individual Commitment to Growth and Life-sharing, Although Visiting is Welcome Too! 161

        Foundational Structure 2: Proximity and Meeting in Person 162

        Foundational Structure 3: Similarity in Lifestyle and in Pursuit 166

        Foundational Structure 4: Frequent Meetings Over Time—In Groups and as Individuals 171

    What Are the Results That May Occur in a Small Group Meeting? 172

    What Should Be Done In Small-Group Gatherings? 174

    Where Should We Meet for Small Groups? 175

    Characteristics of Strong Small Groups 175

Possible Content for Small-Group Meetings 179

The Importance of Eating Together (An Eating Ministry!) 182

How Does Power Evangelism Fit Into Small-Group Discipleship? 184

The Proper Length of Small-Group Meetings 187

Special Small Groups—Family 188

How Many Small Groups Should I Join? 189

Administrative Stuff: When Should I Start a New Small Group? When Should We Disband Our Small Group? How Do We Split? 190

What a Small Group Is Not 191

How to Evangelize 194

The Role of Pastors in Small Groups 194

The Goal of Every Meeting 200

Conclusion 203

End Notes 207

Preface

Bringing People to Christ

In previous writings, I mentioned that a role of kings is to bring the masses to Christ. If you are especially called to the marketplace as a professional or a business owner, this calling belongs to you, not to the leaders of local churches.

In the Church, Christians have stopped asking how we can bring people to Christ. This may be due to lack of results from past attempts or because they do not fully know the saving grace of the gospel. As a result, local churches have become more of a place for individuals to satisfy their personal spiritual longings, in which people tend to lose interest after some time. Local church leaders seem to be focusing on greater worship, sermons, and other administrative activities while neglecting the call of the Great Commission.

Fulfilling the Great Commission has to do with fulfilling the Greatest Commandment, which is to love God and others. My goal for this book is to walk you through the Great Commission and to help make the connection of how history may have distorted our understanding of fulfilling it. Then we will talk about the biblical mandate and practices of Jesus and His disciples. Finally, we will reflect on how we can put our findings into practice. As Christians, we are called to be the salt and light of the world. Let us ask the Holy Spirit for insight and a transformation of our hearts and minds as He guides us through the journey.

Accordingly, this book is laid out in seven sections.

The first section explains what the Great Commission says, or what it means to make disciples.

The second section explains what the gospel says, as there are still misperceptions of the Good News.

The third section provides examples of biblical discipleship that we can reflect on and follow.

The fourth section explains how the Church evolved in history to become what it is today. The intent is to build a case that the church services we hold today may only provide an illusion that we are doing right by God, while it may actually be a faulty cultural trend that persisted over time. Based on our current experiences, we may not actually know how the Church is to operate.

The fifth section recounts great Christian revivals that occurred throughout history where the gospel was shared; this is also known as global missions. This is what truly transformed the world and made Christ known. The revivals all occurred through small groups of believers who stuck together and trusted God together. We are due for another great revival, but it requires changes in our ways of thinking and practice.

The sixth section explains the greatest and highest calling for Christians. As opposed to the discipline of attending services and reading the Scriptures each day, there is a greater calling that is much harder and requires empowerment from God—and that is love.

Finally, the seventh section attempts to provide a practical way of living out a life of discipleship that can occur within local churches (modality) and outside of it (sodality).

During my doctoral studies, I compared the ability to welcome others to Christ through two small groups. One was a long-time gathering of Christian businessmen, and another was a quickly formed small group of pastors and church leaders. There were two key findings:

1. People out in the marketplace are better geared to reach people who do not know Christ. They do this by contact with people in the world, whether they are employees, suppliers, vendors, partners, or even customers.

2. The length of pre-existing relationships, or the depth developed as a result, attracts people who do not believe in Jesus. Needless to say, 50 percent of self-proclaimed non-Christians who took part in the study continued to gather with the Christian businessmen group even after the six-week study was over. One person in particular criticized his friend who invited him, saying, "If the group you invite me to pulls out a guitar and demands that I sing, I may just smash that guitar." He continued to attend meetings beyond the study, and even purchased dinner for everyone at one of the small-group meetings. In fact, at the end of the study, during a debrief, he exclaimed, "If church was like this, I would still be attending." Continual and deep relationships are what enable people to see Jesus, and that is what Christians must focus on.

As a guide for the rest of the reading, I would like to present and explain some terms that I will be using:

Not-yet-Christians. I do not feel comfortable referring to people who do not believe in Christ as non-Christians. The prefix "non" may be construed as an absolute, and readers or listeners might feel that such people, who are also loved by God, are hopelessly lost. Rather, the term *not-yet-Christian* refers to the hope that those who may not yet believe in Jesus soon will. It also refers to the truth that regardless of their current faith, all people will come to bow down before Jesus, recognizing Him as Lord (Philippians 2:9–11).

Church and *local churches*. In this book and elsewhere in my writings, I make a distinction between the two. I capitalize the word *Church* when it refers to the collective body of Jesus Christ. For example, the Church is called to discipleship. This refers to all Christians in the world, including those who must worship in hiding due to political reasons and all who claim to love God. When the word *church* is left in lower case, it refers to local churches. The collection of all local churches would make the global Church.

As you read, if there are quotes or points that interest you, or any questions, join us at ourhighestcalling.com to share them. There you will join with other fellow readers, the staff of Prayer Tents, and the author in exploring related topics together. Let your curiosity grow and may the Holy Spirit lead your heart.

And now, let us begin the journey by reviewing the message and the calling of the Great Commission and how that connects us to our highest calling.

Chapter One

The Great Commission

Therefore, go and make disciples of all the nations, baptizing them in the name of the Father and the Son and the Holy Spirit. Teach these new disciples to obey all the commands I have given you. And be sure of this: I am with you always, even to the end of the age.

Matthew 28:19–20

The Great Commission does not tell us to evangelize, at least not in the way modern Christians understand evangelism. Jesus calls each local church to reach out to their neighbors who do not know Christ; that is what it means to *evangelize*. We are to live lives together with people, even where local bodies of Christ do not exist; that is what is meant by *missions*. We are not called to accomplish this by passing out pamphlets inviting people to come to church and sit for a service, but by discipling them over time, building deeper relationships with one another, and helping them do the same with God; this is called *discipleship*. This points to a lifestyle and spending time with others, or living life together.

Evangelism, missions, and discipleship go hand in hand in both the local and global call directed to all Christians—the Church of Jesus Christ. This includes the local bodies in which Christians are involved (called the *local churches*), as well as all believers in Christ worldwide as a whole (called the *Church*). All Christians are called to make the gospel known, and this cannot occur without understanding and an intentional push toward these three components.

> *Evangelism, missions, and discipleship go hand in hand in both the local and global call directed to all Christians.*

The shrinking attendance in our churches and their uncertainty on how to connect with their neighbors today show that Christians are failing in all three aspects of the Great Commission—that is, in evangelism, missions, and discipleship.

Evangelism, Missions, and Discipleship of Jesus's Disciples

After the resurrection of Jesus, the Holy Spirit came to Jerusalem to bring about a great revival. This same great power came to America, Korea, and even some European countries, where the majority of the people in those countries turned to God in repentance. What has happened to this power? The Great Commission that Jesus left His Church has not been kept. In Matthew 28:18–20, He commanded all His disciples to make other disciples.

> *All Christians are called to make the gospel known.*

Even when Jesus began His ministry, He sought after disciples and focused on training and sending them out. Afterward, He completed His mission, which was to die on the cross for the sins of all mankind. After His resurrection, completing His mission of overcoming sin and death, He did not immediately leave. He spent forty days on earth spending time with His disciples (Acts 1:1–11). Jesus left His disciples the Great Commission—a directive to make disciples—and a promise that He would always be with them (Matthew 28:19–20).

The first thing the disciples did after receiving this directive was to pray, holding on to the promise Jesus had given them (Acts 1:8, 14). Ten days into the prayer, on the day that we call Pentecost, the Holy Spirit came like fire. The key components of discipleship are declaring the gospel of the cross, fervent prayer, and the power of the Holy Spirit and the Word of God (Acts 2; Acts 6:4; 1 Timothy 4:5). The apostle Peter led the crowd that had gathered on the day of Pentecost, performing miracles and declaring the gospel. The result was that about three thousand people turned to God in repentance, beginning what we today call the Church (Acts 2:41). The Church consisted of several small groups of Jesus's disciples that came together. There would be intimate fellowship within these small groups as the believers ate, studied the Word of God, and prayed together (Acts 2:42).

Many Christian leaders often point to the Great Commission to encourage Christians to (1) go forth and (2) evangelize, or tell people about the gospel. There are two issues with this way of thinking:

1. The Great Commission does not tell us to *go and start* something new, but to *continually* live it out.
2. The Great Commission does not tell us to evangelize.

There are no words in the Great Commission that use the Greek root εὐαγγελίζω (*euangelizo*), which refers to bringing the Good News by teaching it.[1] The word εὐαγγέλιον (*euangelion*), actually means "the gospel" or "the Good News." *Evangelize* means to bring that Good News, or to preach it, just as directed in Mark 16:15.

The word *missions* comes from the Latin word *missio*, which comes from the Greek word *apostello*, meaning "to send."[2] Christian missions is to intentionally make plans and send (or be sent) to a different realm, to a different people, and to a place outside one's normal comfort zones to bring (or preach) the gospel. This is an extension of the Great Commission, in which Jesus directed us to go unto all nations (peoples).

Evangelism and missions may seem to be all that is required, but there is one key component missing. If teaching, especially internationally, is all that is needed, why do Christians need to be sent?

> *If teaching is all that is needed, why do Christians need to be sent?*

In our modern day, we certainly have methods to get the teaching out through technology without being physically present.

From the beginning of time, God planned that His people, called the Church, should be a community, a people of God, unified by His leadership. In the same way, even when people are taught by way of the latest technologies, they will not learn or be able to come to faith that endures over time. Rather, true learning and the ability to believe occur *over time* and through others in community.

Additionally, faith is developed over time. This is particularly true when one has held a certain belief for a long time, such as that God does not exist, that God is a Jewish God

> *Faith is developed over time.... It will take time for someone to fully believe.*

and Jesus is just a man, or that God is a Muslim God and Jesus is just another lesser prophet. God can certainly do miracles, and we should never limit what God may do, but in line with His principles, it will take time for someone to fully believe. This is actually the story of Abraham, Joseph, Moses, and other great heroes of faith in the Bible.

What is the term that connotes giving people an environment to be taught in where they can learn over time among others whom they know and respect? Discipleship. Discipleship means to live life together. One cannot be effective in mission work by going one week each year to some foreign land to preach the gospel, because there would be little relational aspect to that (it certainly is better than sending a video or being there for just a few hours, of course). True mission requires effective evangelism that occurs through discipleship where lives are lived together with new peoples. This is why Jesus's last commandment before He left earth was to make disciples. It was only after He made that clear that He added that *making disciples* includes going, baptizing, and teaching, but that is only in the context of relationships formed through discipleship. The discipleship that Jesus modeled and taught is based on life-on-life experiences over time. It does not resemble our current education system, nor how many churches look today.

The Call to Make Disciples

The Commission Jesus gave to all Christians is to make disciples of all people who do not know Him. Amid the busyness boasted of in this world, Christians must make themselves available so that they can disciple anyone seeking to know God. Availability is key in building the discipleship-type relationships that are needed in evangelism and missions.

> *True mission requires effective evangelism that occurs through discipleship.*

The Great Commission recorded in Matthew 28:19–20 includes the necessity for the Church to operate collectively to reach the lost. The only imperative is to *make disciples* as

> *Availability is key in building the discipleship-type relationships that are needed in evangelism and missions.*

Christians are going, baptizing, and teaching for that purpose. Through it all, we must guard our faith and take risks with faith in God.

It is important for Christians to understand that God was targeting us humans when He came to earth as a man to make the atoning sacrifice. His ultimate purpose was not solely to eliminate sin, but rather to rebuild that relationship that was broken because of sin. The gospel is the good news that God is now Immanuel, God with us, and that we can walk with Him as His disciples. Forgiveness of sin was not the ultimate purpose, but was a necessity to accomplish His greater purposes.

During His time on earth, Jesus demonstrated how to make disciples before assigning the same tasks to us. His impact of discipleship can be seen throughout the New Testament. Additionally, the disciples of Jesus, also later called the apostles, are shown to lead small groups of small groups, which eventually led to those small groups joining together as local churches were formed.

Jesus commands His followers to make disciples as they are going, baptizing, and teaching. This can only occur through close hand in hand relationships. Christians must make themselves available, and the Church must make this a practice for the sake of fulfilling the call that Jesus has collectively given to all believers. This may seem difficult or even impossible for some, but God makes all things possible when we trust in Him.

The understanding and execution of Matthew 28:19–20 is foundational to the study of how we, the Church, can improve in our ability to bring people to Christ—that is, to make disciples. *Relationship*s and *availability* of Christians is the key to demonstrating the love of God to others.

The Meaning of Discipleship

Matthew 28:19–20 is the concluding passage of the book of Matthew, where Jesus gathered His core disciples to give the Great Commission before His ascension. Matthew, who authored the book, shows his theological views by placing greater emphasis on the Great Commission than the other Gospel writers do. He summarizes the goal and purpose of God, which is to make disciples.

This promise and execution of the Great Commission begins from the day of Pentecost, when the Holy Spirit was poured out on Jesus's disciples (Acts 2:1–4). From here, the worldwide movement of discipleship began.

The word *disciple* comes from the Greek root μάθετης (*mathates*), meaning to learn or to place into heart (as an example, see Acts 23:27). Being a disciple also means to learn from experience (see Hebrews 5:8). A different-tense Greek word is μανθάνω (*manthano*). It has a meaning that a disciple learns from the master, the one who disciples the disciple, becoming like that person.

In the four Gospels, the twelve who followed Jesus were called disciples. Additionally, Joseph of Arimathea, the one who buried Jesus, is also considered a disciple (Matthew 27:57–60). Though the core disciples came to be called the apostles, other believers were called brothers, believers, or saints, while newly converted believers were called disciples[3] (see Acts 9:1; Acts 13:52; Acts 14:20). Paul (Acts 9:26) and Timothy (Acts 16:1) were also called disciples. Believers were only called Christians after the Antioch church was established (Acts 11:26).[4]

Let us examine verses 19–20 in greater detail:

πορευθέντες οὖν μαθητεύσατε πάντα τὰ ἔθνη,
βαπτίζοντες αὐτοὺς εἰς τὸ ὄνομα τοῦ πατρὸς καὶ τοῦ

> υἱοῦ καὶ τοῦ ἁγίου πνεύματος, διδάσκοντες αὐτοὺς τηρεῖν πάντα ὅσα ἐνετειλάμην ὑμῖν· καὶ ἰδοὺ ἐγὼ μεθ᾽ ὑμῶν εἰμι πάσας τὰς ἡμέρας ἕως τῆς συντελείας τοῦ αἰῶνος.
>
> *Therefore, go and make disciples of all the nations, baptizing them in the name of the Father and the Son and the Holy Spirit. Teach these new disciples to obey all the commands I have given you. And be sure of this: I am with you always, even to the end of the age.*
>
> Matthew 28:19–20

There are several aspects to consider regarding the Great Commission:

- It is the collective calling of all believers, which is the Church, or the body of Jesus Christ.

- It is the call to go after those who do not know God.

- We are to make disciples as we are going, baptizing, and teaching.

- We are to guard our faith and pass it along.

- We must trust God.

It Is the Collective Calling of All Believers, the Church of Jesus Christ

Ἁγίου πνεύματος (*hagiou pnevmatos*) (v. 19)—Holy Spirit. The word *holy* (ἁγίου) is written in plural form, meaning "saints."[5] We can interpret *Holy Spirit* as "the Spirit of the collective saints," or "the Spirit of those who are holy." This, then, means that God is after us, the saints, to work together for His calling. He is not a Spirit who only works *in each of us* individually, but He works in us *collectively* as the Church.

Note also that this Commission was given to Jesus's disciples when they gathered together (see Matthew 28:16). Additionally, this Commission tells us to baptize people in the communion of the Father, Son, and the Holy Spirit. This passage is a commission given to the followers of Jesus—the Church—to fulfill. It is not to individuals, but to a communion of believers.

The name of the Father and the Son and the Holy Spirit points to the unity of God, the three-in-one God. It implies that His power will be with the believers, or united with them, rescuing them from any need. When a person comes to faith in Christ, the three-in-one God, His love and power come upon that person (see Matthew 3:16–17).

The verse, then, can be read this way: "We, the Church of Jesus Christ, the collective people of all local churches, must operate together to reach out to others all around us." The call of the Great Commission is to operate together to reach the world (Matthew 24:14).

> *The call of the Great Commission is to operate together to reach the world.*

It Is the Call to Go After Those Who Do Not Know God.

τὰ ἔθνη (*ta ethni*) (v. 19) means "the nation, people, gentiles."[6] This same word in the NIV is translated in Matthew 6:32 as "pagans." Romans 15:10–11 calls them gentiles. This clearly means that Christians must focus the gospel on people who do not know God instead of becoming churches that are only focused inwardly on their congregations.

The word for "all nations" is the same word used in Matthew 25:32, where all people would have had an opportunity to hear and had the ability to make a decision whether to follow or refuse Jesus as their Lord.

In the Old Testament, the people of Israel were the chosen people of God. Even Jesus followed suit and told His disciples to go after the lost sheep of Israel (Matthew 10:5–6; 15:24). However, after Jesus overcame sin and death, He made a direct path to God without a veiling wall. As a result, Jesus opened up the path to salvation for all. Now both Jews and non-Jews are acceptable to God because of what Jesus has completed (Romans 3:22; Galatians 3:29).

In our modern-day church, the focus has been on the current believing members. This is certainly somewhat necessary; however, if there is no effort to connect with neighbors of other faiths, then the church will either effectively shrink due to attrition, or it must be sustained by transfers from other churches. This means that if churches are simply left alone without further growth, they can only lose membership or have an illusion of sustained numbers due to people coming from other churches. Local churches that gain members who are disgruntled members from other churches, or even from church splits, might rejoice about their seeming increase in membership, but in the body of Christ this is not growth, and it is often something over which to grieve. This is the picture of churches not looking outwardly; unfortunately, this is the picture of many local churches today.

In reality, a person who does not have knowledge about how the church works would probably not attend a worship service on their own because it may be too foreign to them. This is especially true when people already hold a certain belief about God.

It is important to recognize that the church is for Christians, designed to be where Christians meet together to worship God together as they support and encourage one another. The church is often not the appropriate venue to welcome not-yet-Christians. Instead, there needs to be a separate safe space where the not-yet-Christians can be welcomed for a relationship—a small group. Once the lost accept Jesus, they become part of the Church.

> *The church is often not the appropriate venue to welcome not-yet-Christians.*

From a young age, people develop a view about who God is. Children who are taught other beliefs such as Buddhism, Islam, or Hinduism would hold to the worldview of the religion they were taught to believe. This is no different for atheists and agnostics, where they will hold a worldview that God does not or may not exist. They might even believe that they themselves are God, and they will live according to their beliefs.

For such people who have held a certain worldview and practiced such living for many years, it is not reasonable for them to attend a Christian worship service and then instantly change all that they have believed. This means that if a church seeks to reach *those who do not know God*, they must intentionally provide a setting where people can safely come, be who they are, and ask questions *over time* so that they can come to truly understand and experience who God really is and be convinced in their hearts.

We Are to Make Disciples as We Are Going, Baptizing, and Teaching.

The words "make disciples" (v. 19) come from the word μαθητεύσατε (*matheteusate*). It is a command to teach and help others to grow. It means to teach people the gospel and help them grow in their faith (see 2 Timothy 3:14; 4:2–3). Whether regarding Jews who do not know the gospel, or non-Jews who have never heard about it, it means to teach them through life-on-life discipleship until they reach the full and complete standard of Christ (Ephesians 4:13).

Μαθητεύσατε (*matheteusate*) means to make apprentices or disciples. This is the only imperative command Jesus makes in His last

> *We are commanded to make disciples as we are going, baptizing, and teaching.*

guidance to His followers before His departure from earth. In Greek form, Matthew 28:19–20 only has one imperative, which is to "make disciples."[7, 8] *Go*, *baptize*, and *teach* are simply participles that describe how one should go about performing the imperative, which is to *make disciples*. In other words, we are commanded to make disciples as we are going, baptizing, and teaching. Another way to view this is to live out a life (as one is going) that teaches by example (as one is teaching) and baptizes (as one is making disciples).

Making disciples refers to life-on-life relationships. When Jesus called His disciples, they left their occupations because they could not maintain their occupation and live life with Jesus. Jesus's

> *Jesus's command to make disciples means to live with others so that there can be life transformations through life-on-life interactions.*

disciples lived with Him until the day of His death. Jesus's command to make disciples means to live with others, especially those who do not know Him, so that there can be life transformations through life-on-life interactions.

Πορεύομαι (*pareuomai*) (v. 19) means "to go, journey, travel, proceed; depart from; have a destination; and die to self (one's current position)."[9] In terms of evangelism, *going* has to do with adjusting one's own position for the sake of accomplishing the call of Jesus. This word also has implications of leaving one's comfort zone, including the physical land in which one dwells. This is why mission work requires the work and action to be outside of one's homeland. In 1 Corinthians 9:19–23, the apostle Paul says that he bent down toward the dispositions of others so that he could win them to Christ.

This call is for the Christians, and the churches in which they serve, to be willing to take a risk for the sake of connecting with others. It is certainly a risk for pastors of churches to tell the congregation that they may possibly end up in bars and other questionable places because their relationship with those who do not believe in Christ has led them there. It is because of such fear of Christians falling away from their faith that many church leaders advise their members to *avoid people of other faiths*. The church leadership must certainly acknowledge that this is a risky balancing act, yet they must also be aware that by not doing so, they are turning away from the Great Commission.

Matthew 28:20 says, *teach these new disciples to obey all the commands I have given you*. This is a command to educate others about the full message of the Good News. *Teach* is διδάσκω (*didasko*) in the original Greek language. This teaching is not something that is knowledge-based or something that would be taught in a classroom environment, but it is something to be conveyed by sharing lives together through life-sharing over time.

Διδάσκω (*didasko*) means to teach and instruct, but there is a deeper intention than our modern-day thinking of having a thirty-minute lecture on a specific topic.[10] This verse refers to both instructive and hands-on guidance. This word is used when someone is taught to play a musical instrument. One cannot become a musician just by listening to many lectures about it. It requires close, one-on-one, hands-on teaching that is continuous over time. After multiple connections, the students become adept enough to learn and grow on their own. The mentor may then meet with the students less frequently, but they will connect over time because a relationship has formed through their training.

Διδάσκω (*didasko*) then follows, pointing to how to go about making disciples. Over the past century, evangelical organizations with good intentions came up with methods to speed up and objectively measure people coming to Christ. Their easy-to-understand methods were invaluable in enabling people to understand the Bible message. However, the proliferation of these methodologies removed discipleship, and Christians were out in the streets to "save" many. Without discipleship, these methods led many people to believe they were Christians who had eternal life through Christ, even though they did not truly know God. The gospel can certainly be explained through brief interactions, but the changing of a person's way of living and coming to faith in God involves time, as it is something that only God is able to do in His time and in His way. Discipleship is life-on-life over time.

Nabeel Qureshi was raised as a devout Muslim with a set of beliefs developed from his birth. In his book *Seeking Allah, Finding Jesus*, he shares his experience of questioning his Islamic faith and the years and interactions it took for him to trust in Jesus as Lord.[11] Whether a person is an atheist, agnostic, or from another religion, it will take time to question, learn the differences in views, and commit to understand what the person needs to leave behind. For some, it may even be rejection from family—or possibly worse.

Therefore, evangelism *is not just bringing someone to church*. Many church leaders, for sake of attendance or possibly because they do not understand evangelism, tell the congregation to bring more people to the church. Although the church leaders might certainly have good intentions, attending a church service may make the new person feel uncomfortable in a non-relational setting. A worship service is the environment for Christians to worship God, and it is less suitable for not-yet-Christians, though we should not limit God as to where He would encounter the people whom He loves.

We live in busy times today, when many "believers" allot one or two hours for the Lord's Day worship service each week. That service often concludes the "church" experience *tasks* for the week. However, for evangelism to truly occur, certain things

> *For evangelism to truly occur, certain things must exist: (1) a comfortable setting for learning, (2) people being who they are, (3) observing other believers, and (4) asking questions.*

must exist, such as a comfortable setting where people can be discipled, a safe place where they can come as they are, the ability to observe what it means to be a community that worships the God of love, and the freedom to ask questions.

These are the benefits of outside-the-church gatherings and interactions. This is what is known as home churches or small groups. Done effectively, this will open the door for many to come and explore.

Evangelism is not a spectator sport. The Great Commission says to go, which means to travel and to depart from one's current position; it is an active role that requires intention. It is the basis of discipleship, in which Christians are to give up what is important to them (die to self), including time and money, so that they will be available to those who are willing to hear and learn about God.

A command to baptize—βαπτίζοντες (*baptizontes*)—during the discipleship process is also given.[12] Baptism signifies that the person has initiated his or her faith in Christ in front of other believers. It signifies commitment to grow in faith.[13] In the Early Church, it was a public declaration that the person was committing their old self to death, which included renouncing all sin, dying to self, and recognizing themselves as new creations in Christ.

However, baptism does not equate to salvation or eternal life. It is a starting commitment, and as frail people, we can turn away from God even after this stage without developing a firm faith in God (see John 6:66). Salvation and eternal life are dependent on faith (John 3:16; Romans 1:17), which comes from God as a gift to us (Ephesians 2:8–9).

Baptism is either immersion of a person under water or a simple cleansing (see 2 Kings 5:14; Mark 7:14; Luke 11:38); both are valid. The key importance is that the person publicly announces and confesses their faith. One becomes a child of God by faith. Baptism, though, is a physical act of appearing in front of other believers to publicly confess one's faith in Christ.

> *One becomes a child of God by faith.*

This is a significant message: as not-yet-believing people dwell among believers, they can come to know God. Baptism, a commitment to follow Jesus and to be His disciple, occurs through life-on-life walking with Christians. In other words, it is through deep relationships that people really encounter Christ, and not through just attending church services.

Discipleship involves life-on-life living together where the person leading the disciple and the disciple are *near and working together over time*. This practice has been reduced, or even eliminated, in many churches today due to the world's promotion of being busy and an increase in hyper-connectivity. Many so-called Christians, being no different from the people who do not believe in Jesus, think of Christianity as a religion defined by faithful attendance at worship services on Sundays. However, the call to *make disciples while going, baptizing, and teaching* is for all believers, and this involves leaving one's comfort zone and giving up time and/or other resources for the growth of others (which in turn causes them to grow too!).

We Are to Guard Our Faith and Pass It Along.

Τηρέω (*tireo*), often translated as "to observe and obey," has the meaning "to keep firm and guard."[14] It means that Christians ought to preserve the things that God has taught them by passing their learnings along, just as one teaches their disciples. It also means to pay attention to what God has taught them. This word has implications for the current follower of Christ, as well as the responsibility for us to pass along the message.

This word points to a believer's need to live a life worthy of being a follower of Christ. The person can be a good role model for others by simply paying attention to what

> *Christians ought to preserve the things that God has taught them by passing their learnings along.*

God has already taught them and by living according to those truths. As people demonstrate Christlikeness in their lives, others may be inspired to live in a similar way. If a person is willing to pass along the message to another person who is interested, and will also work with that person to develop that kind of lifestyle, it is called discipleship. Therefore, observing and obeying τηρέω (*tireo*) has implications for life modeling, which translates to discipleship.

We Are to Trust God.

Μετά (*meta*) (v. 20) means "in the midst of" or "together with."[15] It means that as we go forth in our living, God will be with us. In one sense, Jesus may have said this in order to comfort all believers as His last message to us before His ascension; however, we can also recognize that Jesus intended to say what is most important for His followers as we go about doing what may be difficult, but is most important—that is, making disciples.

It means to take the risk and go forward with the knowledge that God is with us. Jesus challenged His disciples, including you and me, to embrace and carry out a complex task, which is to make disciples of all nations. Since the call is so vast, many Christians and churches do not partake in this call, perhaps thinking that someone else will carry out the work (this is called the "bystander effect" in social psychology[16]). Christians, including those in church leadership, often do not intentionally plan to connect with people who do not believe in Jesus, thinking instead that evangelism is something that happens by chance.

Jesus being with us, μετά (*meta*), impels us to rely on God to work when we go about the "risky" activities of connecting with people who do not believe in Christ. It is indeed God, not us, who will save those whom He will save (Hebrews 7:25; Romans 9:15–16, 22–24). The listener's ability to believe in the message at a specific point in time and circumstance is also something God is managing (see Luke 24:13–32). Even the words that we would speak, perhaps a word of knowledge or just simple explanations about why we believe what we do, is again something for which God takes responsibility (Matthew 10:19; Mark 13:11; Luke 12:11–12).

I am with you always, even to the end of the age has implication until the day Jesus returns to take His followers home (Matthew 24:14).

Until then, Jesus protects His followers and even empowers them by sending the Holy Spirit (John 14:16; 15:26; 16:7). Jesus will protect, guide, and provide for all who place their trust in Him. This promise was fulfilled at Pentecost (Acts 2:1–4), leading to worldwide mission movements. It is only through the provision, help, and guidance of the Holy Spirit that we can partake in such great callings and reach people all over the world as Jesus directed.

What Christians are left with, then, is to simply obey the command to make disciples while going, baptizing, and teaching in the name of Jesus to the people who do not yet believe in Him. This requires an intention to live Christlike lives worthy of being imitated, along with a willingness to die to one's own needs in order to disciple and care for others over time. Through all this, Jesus will be with us, and we do not need to worry; instead, we must simply obey and trust, pressing on in walking with others in discipleship.

The Great Commission and Jesus/Disciples Doing Discipleship

The Commission Jesus gave to all Christians is to make disciples of all people who do not know Him. Amid the busyness boasted of in this

> *Busy people cannot be available.*
> *Busy people cannot love in action.*

world, Christians must make themselves available so that they can disciple anyone seeking to know God. Availability is key in building discipleship relationships that are connected to evangelism and missions. Busy people cannot be available. Busy people cannot love in action.

The Great Commission recorded in Matthew 28:19–20 intends for the Church to operate collectively to reach the lost. The only imperative is to make disciples while going, baptizing, and teaching. Through it all, we must guard our faith and take risks with faith in God.

It is important for Christians to understand that God was targeting us when He came to earth as a human to make the atoning sacrifice. His ultimate purpose was to rebuild the relationship that was broken by sin. The good news—the gospel—is that God sent Jesus, Immanuel with us, and we can walk with Him.

During His time on earth, Jesus demonstrated how to make disciples before He assigned that same task to us. The impact of discipleship can be seen throughout the New Testament. Additionally, the disciples of Jesus, also called the apostles, are shown to lead small groups of small groups, which eventually led to those groups joining together to form local churches.

Jesus commands us to make disciples by going, teaching, and baptizing. This can only occur through close hand in hand relationships. Christians must make themselves available, and the Church must make this a practice for the sake of fulfilling the call that Jesus has given to all believers collectively. This may seem difficult or even impossible for some, but God makes all things possible when we trust in Him.

The understanding and execution of Matthew 28:19–20 is foundational to the study of how we, the Church, can improve in our ability to evangelize—that is, to make disciples. Relationship and availability of Christians is the key in demonstrating the love of God to others.

Small-Group Reflections

1. How do you evangelize today?
2. What are some changes you may need to make in your life in order to make disciples as Jesus commands?

Chapter Two

The Good News Explained

If there is no fight in you, you have no faith.
The gospel without power is not the gospel. [17]

—Samuel S. Goebel

As followers of Christ, we need to know the message of the Good News that Jesus brings. Discipleship cannot occur without encountering Jesus, for this is how we experience this Good News, which is also called the gospel. The gospel is simply the truth that we can have a direct relationship with God because He has sent Jesus to us to take care of the issues that prevented us from doing so. Jesus's death on the cross and His resurrection gave us forgiveness from sins, and now our God dwells in us through His Spirit (the Holy Spirit) and guides us in our paths to what is best.

This gospel message must be correctly understood and communicated in order to fulfill the call of the Great Commission. Discipleship is helping people understand and live out the deeper relationship with God that is available because of what God has done for us. The gospel does not simply end with Jesus's death and resurrection that leads us to heaven, as many Christians misunderstand. It is *living with Jesus*, or discipleship, that God has enabled us to live out.

Unfortunately, since many people have a cheap understanding of the gospel, such as believing that certain acts such as attending church on Sundays or repeating a specific prayer justify us, we have many so-called "almost Christians" who see Christianity as a religious act to appease an angry God. Just as a person needs to continue to mow the yard to prevent an ugly outgrowth, "almost Christians" squeeze religious activities into their lives, activities such as attending church, as a maintenance activity to try to keep themselves "saved." Their relationship with God is not their highest priority, but rather it is something that is *done and accomplished by them in order to stay saved.*

Therefore, clarification of the gospel message is necessary. The purpose of salvation brought to us by God is to mend the broken relationship with God so that we may hear Him and walk with Him. Many people recognize the gospel to be this way: God saw the problem of sin that He did not like, so He sent Jesus to die for our sins. This is certainly correct, but the emphasis is on the wrong object.

The gospel cannot end with just the forgiveness. The reason Jesus died was to *bridge the broken relationship*, not to focus on the sin. The goal was to take away the issue of sin so that our focus would be back on God. Though it is certainly good news that our sin problem has been resolved, that is not the complete reason why God chose to intercede; that is not the gospel.

> *The reason Jesus died was to bridge the broken relationship.*

The gospel, the Good News, is that we can have a relationship with God! Through what Jesus has done, we now have the Holy Spirit, who enables us to believe and understand the guidance from God. He does this by first enabling a person to *begin to believe*. Along the way, He will strengthen their faith so that they would have unwavering faith in Him.[18]

The variations of the "sinner's prayer" that has been used by evangelicals during the past few centuries has focused on forgiveness of sins, which has been taught to immediately provide salvation or eternal life.[19] Though forgiveness of sin plays a part, salvation and eternal life have always been a result of faith or the person's believing or trusting in God:

> *For this is how God loved the world: He gave his one and only Son, so that everyone who* **believes** *in him will not perish but have eternal life.*
>
> John 3:16
> (bold added)

> *This Good News tells us how God makes us right in his sight. This is accomplished from start to finish by faith. As the Scriptures say, "It is* **through faith** *that a righteous person has life."*
>
> Romans 1:17
> (bold added)

However, this faith does not come from us. The faith to believe in God comes from Him too. It is not something we start up one day out of our own will. If that were the case, then we could boast that we believed in God on our own, and as a result, we could demand that we are worthy of salvation (see Ephesians 2:8–9).

Hebrews 11:1 says that faith *is the evidence of things we cannot see.* As opposed to laws of physics, which we can see and verify to believe, faith in the invisible God requires His intervention. When He shows Himself to us, that is when a person can begin to believe. That is why the Bible points to God's initiation of salvation for those He has chosen:

> *So I want you to know that no one speaking by the Spirit of God will curse Jesus, and no one can say Jesus is Lord, except by the Holy Spirit.*
>
> 1 Corinthians 12:3

> *When the Spirit of truth comes, **he will guide you into all truth**. He will not speak on his own but will tell you what he has heard. He will tell you about the future.*
>
> John 16:13
> (bold added)

> *Because of the privilege and authority God has given me, I give each of you this warning: Don't think you are better than you really are. Be honest in your evaluation of yourselves, measuring yourselves **by the faith God has given us**.*
>
> Romans 12:3
> (bold added)

> *For God knew his people in advance, and he chose them to become like his Son, so that his Son would be the firstborn among many brothers and sisters. And having chosen them, he called them to come to him. And having called them, he gave them right standing with himself. And having given them right standing, he gave them his glory.*
>
> Romans 8:29–30

Therefore, it is important to recognize and communicate to the many people who go to church every week that *they might not be going to heaven*. Their religious works of attendance do not make them righteous or faithful. The same goes for those who have recited the "sinner's prayer" in the past. This may also be true for some who have gone forward during altar calls at a revival service. Their salvation would only be recognized by the depth of their relationship with God that begins with faith that comes from God.

> *Not everyone who calls out to me, "Lord! Lord!" will enter the Kingdom of Heaven. Only those who actually do the will of my Father in heaven will enter.*
>
> Matthew 7:21

The only way to obtain faith in God is by His grace. To grow in it is to begin with that gift and continue to remain in Him, the perfecter of our faith (Hebrews 12:2).

Some believe that the Bible encourages the use of the "sinner's prayer" based on Romans 10:9–13:

> *If you openly declare that Jesus is Lord and believe in your heart that God raised him from the dead, you will be saved. For it is by believing in your heart that you are made right with God, and it is by openly declaring your faith that you are saved. As the Scriptures tell us, "Anyone who trusts in him will never be disgraced." Jew and Gentile are the same in this respect. They have the same Lord, who gives generously to all who call on him. For "Everyone who calls on the name of the Lord will be saved."*

However, these verses will make sense when they are read through the lens that the faith required to trust in God is a gift that comes from God. Specifically, one can only begin to declare that

> *We are made right with God because God gives us the faith to trust in Him.*

Jesus is Lord once the person believes, which begins with God. How can one believe in their heart that God raised Jesus, or anyone for that matter, from the dead? God must intervene and demonstrate who He is to the person. We are made right with God because God gives us the faith to trust in Him.

Finally, who can call on the Lord? It is someone who has faith in Him and knows Him. This is like a child calling out for his mother or father; the child would not call out "mother" or "father" to a stranger he does not know. So then, without supernatural initiation of our faith, we cannot begin the journey of faith.

Even John Wesley once professed that he "felt [his] heart strangely warmed." He wrote, "I felt I did trust in Christ, Christ alone, for salvation; and an assurance

> *People can think they are Christians, and even hold church positions, but not be saved.*

was given me that He had taken away my sins, even mine, and saved me from the law of sin and death."[20] Luther Oconer, assistant professor of United Methodist Studies at United Theological Seminary, wrote to me in an email that this was Wesley's experience of "justifying faith." After realizing that it was what was missing in his life, Wesley embarked on a two-year quest to experience it, until finally he experienced it in a religious society meeting at Aldersgate Street in London. This faith, as Wesley's experience has shown, is something that may be acquired over time, and the approach of leading a seeker through the "sinner's prayer" may prove to be insufficient for a person to truly believe in God.[21] Additionally, Wesley probably considered himself as a Christian since he even held the title of a pastor and spoke about God in front of congregations. This shows that many people can think they are Christians, and even hold church positions, but not be saved.

In the same email mentioned above, Professor Oconer, responding to my question about whether the sinner's prayer was acceptable in the Wesleyan's view of salvation, replied:

> Your concern about the sinner's prayer is actually the very thing I'm trying to address because it cheapens the gospel. The sinner's prayer (as well as altar call) is an American invention brought about by the prevalent "short cut" approach in American evangelical culture during the nineteenth century. During Wesley's time, they didn't have that. That came later during the second great awakening in America with the introduction of the mourner's bench (like a form of altar call).
>
> During Wesley's time, people gained saving faith in Jesus mostly in the context of discipleship, and not as a result of a one-off encounter or a 10-minute conversation. Also, Wesley did not teach repentance as a requirement for justification or eternal life. There is only one requirement for him—it's saving faith in Jesus, or what we call justification by faith, or justifying faith (Romans 5:1). If repentance is the requirement, then salvation depends on us and not God. That is why it is by faith alone. This faith is not our doing; it is God's grace. It is a gift from God (Ephesians 2:8). But how do we know we have saving faith or justifying faith? We can know through the witness of the Spirit (Romans 8:16). Saving faith is not simply gained by reciting some magic formula. Because faith, according to Wesley, is not simply an

assent or agreeing to something. It involves the heart or our whole affection.

So then, what is the biblical way a person can be saved if tracts that include the "sinner's prayer" are not the answer? The answer lies back in Jesus's Great Commission in Matthew 28: it is the command to make disciples.

Discipleship requires commitment from individuals to be together over a period of time. The problem in the twenty-first century is the trend of busyness—something that people believe is something to be proud of.[22] With social media in a hyper-connected society, kids even at the age of five are preoccupied and want to be left alone with their electronics.[23] With teens constantly having to check their updates on Facebook, Twitter, emails, and chat applications, it is no wonder why people no longer have time for anything else.

Pastor Sam Hwang from Christ Life Church gave a presentation at the Ambassador's Conference 2017 stating that pastors are ineffective because they do not have margin on time.[24] He was pointing to the fact that ministry to individuals, which is how discipleship works, requires time; however, because there are apparently so many things that take up the pastors' time, they cannot tend to their original focus of shepherding people.

This is why *discipleship* is no longer a term used in today's churches. It is no longer understood. That is also the reason why many churches are in decline and struggling.

> *True evangelism requires people to relate, life-on-life, based on a mutual commitment to grow.*

Evangelism, or discipleship, seems to now be a lost art. True evangelism requires people to relate, life-on-life, based on a mutual commitment to grow. A Christian must model a life for others to follow, and they must help those who desire to grow to follow, not from afar, but in close proximity, while giving time to the learner as needed.

Discipleship Requires Relationships That Are Dependent on the Learner

Discipleship is a relationship between individuals that is cultivated over time with the intent to know God more. This definition applies both to people who do not know God but are interested in learning about Him, as well as those who know God and desire to grow deeper in Him by knowing Him more.

The mistake many Christians make about evangelism is establishing activities and their timing around their needs and availability. For example, a church might have a program to send people out to the local supermarkets at 3 p.m. after the Lord's Day service, since that is the time the congregation members are readily together and available. They can go to a supermarket and have tracts available with the name and contact information of the church they attend.

> *The mistake many Christians make about evangelism is establishing activities and their timing around their needs and availability.*

God brings people to faith at different times, often through life experiences, at any hour of any day. It is at those times that they would seek someone to help them meet God, but because evangelism only occurs at special pre-planned bursts, the people who are seeking do not receive help from these Christians who are busy when the seekers are longing for help or guidance from God.

Another reason why modern-day evangelism fails is because Christians no longer see evangelism as making relationships, but rather see it as a goal-oriented activity—just like work in the modern world. Their metrics may be for someone to repeat the "sinner's prayer" or to get them to their church.

> *Christians no longer see evangelism as making relationships, but rather see it as a goal-oriented activity.*

Several people who desire their local church to grow in membership have asked, "*What do I need to do* in order to get more people to church?"[25] The problem with this question is that it begins with the mindset of needing to do something and have activities in order to produce results. When they are told that they need to go meet more people and form relationships with them, they are often taken aback with thoughts that there must be another way that perhaps is quicker and more efficient.

Accordingly, pastors who do not understand that evangelism requires building relationships may tell their congregations to go out to popular places for the sake of evangelism. The congregation may rightly follow out of obedience to their shepherd, but it may be of greater benefit for pastors and the believers in his care to better understand the Great Commission of Jesus so that they will benefit through true discipleship.

Evangelism is building relationships. It is about being available. It is walking with others hand in hand through life together. It takes much commitment and sacrifice of time to truly win a person to Christ. It cannot be done over a short time

> *Evangelism is building relationships. . . . walking with others hand in hand through life together.*

by simply passing out tracts and asking someone to recite a special prayer.

Being available to the people who are interested can be seen in Paul's life in his letter to the church of Corinth:

> *Even though I am a free man with no master, I have become a slave to all people to bring many to Christ. When I was with the Jews, I lived like a Jew to bring the Jews to Christ. When I was with those who follow the Jewish law, I too lived under that law. Even though I am not subject to the law, I did this so I could bring to Christ those who are under the law. When I am with the Gentiles who do not follow the Jewish law, I too live apart from that law so I can bring them to Christ. But I do not ignore the law of God; I obey the law of Christ. When I am with those who are weak, I share their weakness, for I want to bring the weak to Christ. Yes, I try to find common ground with everyone, doing everything I can to save some. I do everything to spread the Good News and share in its blessings.*
>
> 1 Corinthians 9:19–23

Paul made himself available to anyone in just the way they needed Christ while holding on to the heart and pursuit of bringing them to Christ. Consider his wording: *I lived like*, *I have become*, *I too lived*, and *When I am with*. These words are not short-burst projects to accomplish, but a living-out over time to win the hearts of others and make disciples.

Paul also shares in his letters to the Christians in Corinth that his intent is not just to give instructions, but to truly spend time with them in fellowship:

> *This time I don't want to make just a short visit and then go right on. I want to come and stay awhile, if the Lord will let me. In the meantime, I will be staying here at Ephesus until the Festival of Pentecost. There is a wide-open door for a great work here, although many oppose me.*
>
> 1 Corinthians 16:7–9

> *You should imitate me, just as I imitate Christ.*
>
> 1 Corinthians 11:1

Paul also exhorts them to know with certainty that they are believing correctly:

> *Let me now remind you, dear brothers and sisters, of the Good News I preached to you before. You welcomed it then, and you still stand firm in it. It is this Good News that saves you if you continue to believe the message I told you—unless, of course, you believed something that was never true in the first place.*
>
> 1 Corinthians 15:1–2

> *Examine yourselves to see if your faith is genuine. Test yourselves. Surely you know that Jesus Christ is among you; if not, you have failed the test of genuine faith.*
>
> 2 Corinthians 13:5

Prayer Tents, a Christian mission organization, summarizes the gospel this way:

> God created us, starting from Adam and Eve, to have a close relationship with us.

However, there was a problem with disobedience to God, called sin, that separated us from God. People tried to bridge this gap, but it was not possible because of the perfect standard of God. God had a plan to resolve this issue, because this was something only He could resolve.

This plan was to restore our relationship by giving us the hearts that enable us to love God and follow His commands (Deuteronomy 30:6, 10). It would not be out of duty, but our hearts and actions would be aligned to what God has in mind.

The end result of this plan would be a continual relationship with God—He would be with us and would be our guide. He does this by sending His Spirit to dwell in our hearts.

Who can receive the Holy Spirit so that they may dwell with the Lord at all times? We must become a sanctuary for God; that is, we must be holy and pure before God so that He may dwell in our hearts.

This was the original problem when sin came into play, remember? For this reason, God Himself came down to earth (the Son, whose name is Jesus) to make a permanent sacrifice for all. Anyone who believes in Jesus and what He has done will be considered as if they have no sin, which means they are pure and acceptable before God (John 3:16; Romans 12:1; 1 Corinthians 3:16–17; 6:19; Hebrews 10:1–23; 1 Peter 2:4–5).

Anyone who has the Holy Spirit living in them is said to be born again with the Spirit of God. We will live eternally with God with joy and reign over many things, as it was intended in the original Garden.

Then, the Good News of the Bible is this: Believe in God, and you will have a relationship with Him. He will enable you to joyfully love Him and follow His commands. He will guide you every step of the way, and you will not need to worry about anything in life. Your spirit will be born again with His, and you will live eternally with Him.[26]

This summary of the gospel includes the truth that God provides the faith, and it is not something we do. Through the faith that He gives, He enables us to grow into a state that is acceptable to commune with Him.

Small-Group Reflections

1. How does the gospel, the Good News of Jesus Christ, affect your everyday living?
2. How is your relationship with Jesus? How goes your soul?

Chapter Three

How Jesus and His Disciples Made Other Disciples

You don't impact masses; you impact individuals.[27]

How Jesus Did Discipleship

Jesus called Christians to make disciples, and He demonstrated it through His ministry so that we could imitate Him. First, the disciples of Jesus were simply people who had interest in God. Even though the Bible does not explicitly say why Simon Peter, Andrew, James, and John were able to drop what they were doing and immediately follow Jesus at His request (Matthew 4:18–22), we can surmise that they were not satisfied with where they were in life, and perhaps they wanted something more. There was an *interest* or *desire* to find out about God.[28]

This initiation is something only God is able to do, and He continues to initiate in the same way today. Many young adults, though many church leaders may not see this, are currently seeking for life guidance and are wondering if there is something more. Christians need to be able to recognize when God is working, and they need to welcome such people to a community where they can observe, ask questions, and grow.[29]

Jesus began His *small group* by gathering such people who had some interest in knowing God. They certainly did not know God, nor were they people of great stature or recognition. Nonetheless,

Jesus taught—διδάσκω (*didasko*)—and discipled—μαθητεύω (*mathetevo*)—them, and they went about transforming their culture and the way people of those times thought (see the book of Acts and other writings in the New Testament), and their impact persists even to our day. The Christian faith began with Jesus and His small group, which in turn developed other small groups. That one small group has now formed what is known as the Church today.

That explains how Jesus started to bring people to become disciples, but how did He go about *making them into disciples*? He walked with them, showed them, and taught them hand in hand. To illustrate this, we can see what Jesus did with His disciples by following the account from Matthew:

> *Christian faith began with Jesus and His small group, which in turn developed other small groups.*

- He exemplified teaching crowds (Matthew 5–7). Note that the message Jesus shared to the public was valuable to the disciples too. The disciples likely saw Him in His preparation and execution of the work. The disciples probably ate with Jesus, asked questions, and had other insights in close proximity with Him.

- He exemplified a life of miracles while teaching that it occurs by faith. This included healing a leper, a servant of a Roman soldier, and many others. Jesus taught them to love, to care for, and to have compassion for others (Matthew 8:1–17; 9:19–34; 15:21–31; 18:24–34).

- He taught them about the costs of placing faith in God (Matthew 8:18–22).

- He taught them about persevering in faith in God for anything in this world instead of being afraid of things (Matthew 8:23–27). This is also evident when Jesus stands up against leaders who understood or taught about God incorrectly (Matthew 23).

- He exemplified a life of miracles, teaching that this can happen to glorify God. It does not have to depend on the faith of the recipient, but when God is doing something and when believers see this and follow along in faith, God may act and demonstrate His power in healing and miracles (Matthew 8:28–9:8; 12:9–13, 22–37).

- He demonstrated and showed that many people need God, and He taught them to seek God first and to seek Him for more workers while they continued the work of Jesus as they discipled others (Matthew 9:35–10:42).

- He taught His followers to center on who God is instead of trying to impress people with miracles. Miracles are only to occur as God intends. Jesus demonstrated to His disciples the need to be ready to teach and not to follow the requests of the crowds (Matthew 12:39–45; 16:1–4).

- He taught them to share stories so the listeners can understand the deeper message (Matthew 13; 18:12–14, 21–35; 21:28–22:14; 25).

- He taught and demonstrated that there is nothing impossible for God (Matthew 14).

- He taught that God is interested in who we are—in our inner persons and our souls—more than in what we do or who we look like on the outside (Matthew 15).

These are simple examples of what Jesus did together with—μετά (*meta*)—His disciples. The call, then, is to imitate Jesus in discipling and teaching others in close proximity and sharing lives together. That is how we make disciples, and that is true evangelism.

> *The call is to imitate Jesus in discipling and teaching others in close proximity and sharing lives together. That is how we make disciples, and that is true evangelism.*

How Jesus's Disciples Did Discipleship

The Bible also shows how the disciples of Jesus, later called the apostles, discipled others. Though we do not see the same kinds of small groups led by them, we can see how they built small groups after small groups.

After the Holy Spirit was given to them, they experienced the greatest revival that had occurred up to that time. The first few chapters of Acts tell chapter after chapter about thousands of people coming to believe in God. When this occurred, the apostles had the charge of discipling all those believers who had recently come to find interest or need in God. Though it is not explicitly shared in the Scriptures, we can surmise that the sudden growth of small groups shown in Acts 2:42–47 is a result of guidance and teaching from the apostles.[30]

The result of this great outburst of new initiates of faith was due to small-group gatherings. Verse 44 says that the believers gathered in one place to share their belongings with others. This cannot be a picture of a multitude because there would not be enough for one or two people to give to hundreds of people. Additionally, when there is a large crowd, people do not have the ability to dialogue and understand the needs of individuals. This verse shows that there was a sharing between people within small groups who dialogued with

> *When there is a large crowd, people do not have the ability to dialogue and understand the needs of individuals.*

each other to understand how they can help one another. They worked together and gave to each other in order to meet immediate needs so they could go to God together.

Then verses 44–45 talk about an outburst of multiple small groups that were under the guidance of the apostles, focusing on the four topics mentioned in verse 42, namely learning about God, sharing lives together, eating together, and prayer. They also worshipped (v. 47) and were filled with joy (v. 46).

Verse 46 shares a bit more about the arrangement. People worshipped together at the *temple*. Though this word is literally translated as "temple," the gathering occurred outside

> *God not only works inside the church, but may also operate in even greater power outside the church.*

the temple. The reason is that the temple was generally for temple administrators and leaders. No women or gentiles would be allowed inside. Besides, there would not be enough space for all the people to fit inside these buildings. That is why the New International Version translates this as "temple courts." This can be seen as how God not only works inside the church, but may also operate in even greater power outside the church.

People worshipping at the temple courts points to gatherings of multiple small groups, or what might be similar to big gatherings in our churches today. Within local churches, there must be small groups, as shown in the latter part of verse 46, where people met in their homes to eat and share lives together while filling the needs of one another. People were willing to give what they had, and they invited others, even covering the cost of food and giving their time for the sake of others.

The disciples of Jesus began the administration of these small groups and continued with their teachings (Acts 3–5). However, being involved in administration, they could not stay focused on their primary goal of teaching, so they eventually delegated this task to others (Acts 6).

Discipleship is about person-to-person, life-on-life connections. Christians who have a relationship with God can share the same with others who are interested in God. Through such life-on-life interactions over time, others can see and experience God in action.

> *Christians who have a relationship with God can share the same with others who are interested in God. Through such life-on-life interactions over time, others can see and experience God in action.*

Sadly, such infrastructure to welcome others is often missing in modern-day churches. We cannot continue to expand more worship services with the view that we are not devoted enough; rather, we need a place where people can individually grow from *where they are* and *along the way*. Just like the Church shown in Acts 2, the small groups can be a place where Christians can share with others what God has given them, sharing their resources of time and money to care for the needs of others as they come to know them and their needs deeply in person.

The Gospel and Intercession of Believers

It is God's prerogative to bring about salvation for anyone because He is the supplier of faith that enables people to believe in God. That being the case, what can Christians do to help when people ask about God with a desire to know Him? We can welcome them to community and pray with them while having faith in God for the outcome.

> *We can welcome them to community and pray with them while having faith in God for the outcome.*

When God begins to work in the life of someone to bring about the initial interest, we want to welcome such people into our loving and personally growing small groups where they can freely share their concerns and their lives. Over time, the interested people will have received the opportunity to gain information about God, find answers to their questions, and perhaps even experience some miracles of God among them, while they also experience the generosity of other believers in meeting their needs (see Acts 2:42–46).

> *Over time, the interested people will have received the opportunity to gain information about God, find answers to their questions, and perhaps even experience some miracles of God among them, while they also experience the generosity of other believers in meeting their needs.*

Changing one's faith takes time, and it is important at this phase to enable relationships so that the person can always ask questions and feel comfortable during this journey.

As believers, assuming we are aligned with God in a desire to bring people into a relationship with God (Ezekiel 18:23; 1 Timothy

2:4; 2 Peter 3:9), *what can a Christian do* if it is solely God's decision to bring about salvation? The answer is that we can pray for them.

The prerogative, of course, still rests with God, but as children of God we have the right to come to Him with any request, just as children can do with their human parents (John 1:12; Galatians 4:7; 1 John 3:10). We can intercede for them (Galatians 6:2; Ephesians 6:18; 1 Timothy 2:1, 4), seek God's will (1 John 5:14), and communicate what we hear from God to comfort the person, which includes words of knowledge or prophetic messages. Through such prayers, God may demonstrate His love toward them by meeting their needs, giving them guidance, and even bringing about healing (James 5:15–16).

James 5:15–16 requires a little more attention. Προσεύχομαι (*proseuchomai*)—prayer—which has the meaning "to ask or plead with God," is used as both a noun and a verb in these verses to imply that we can pray to bring about forgiveness and healing for someone else. A person who is seeking God may be able to experience God as Christians pray for them and with them.

Prayer for others is important because it is a way that we can help believers who are going through a rough patch, or we can even help not-yet-believers by comforting them with the guidance that God might share through us. That is why prayer is one of the four items listed in Acts 2:42 that discipleship small groups ought to maintain when together with one another.

Additionally, Jesus taught His disciples that *many people need God*, but relatively few people minister to them (Matthew 9:37–38). He then tells His disciples to ask, or pray to, the Lord of the Harvest to send more workers. In that sense, when we intercede for others that they will truly experience God and be reborn with His Spirit, we are effectively asking God to send us more ministers of His grace. As

God fills them, they become our brothers and sisters who also respond to the call of the Great Commission together.

Small-Group Reflections

1. How do you practice discipleship?
2. How do people around you know that you are a disciple of Jesus?

Chapter Four

History of the Gospel, Evangelism, and Missions

Remember Christ's disciples. They rowed their heavy ships to shore, then abandoned everything to follow Christ.

—Elfric of Eynsham

There have been shifts in methods of evangelism over the years, and it no longer resembles the methods taught in the Scriptures. Since the times of the Early Church, as recorded in the book of Acts, many political and cultural changes affected how the Church and its clergy operated. As a result, it is very possible that the operations of the local churches we see today may not be what Jesus desired to see. All Christians must reflect on this matter and consider where God calls each of us to go individually and collectively as the global Church and how we ought to operate.

The purpose of this section is to provide the history of how the Great Commission and the operations of the Church have been practiced, and how that has evolved over time. How the gospel message has been understood and how that understanding has evolved over time will also be discussed. During the past two millennia, people have had different understandings of how they could be saved.

The history will show how Christianity has now become a passive religion to many people and will emphasize the need for a reform—a return to discipleship—that will bring us back to the gospel that Jesus taught.

Then the focus will shift to how John Wesley, the founder of the Methodist Church, implemented the Great Commission into practice in church settings. This implementation, called "class meetings," is how the Methodist community of faith has grown to 80 million people worldwide today. Putting the Great Commission into practice using similar methods may be the path to producing faithful disciples of Jesus.

The Great Commission as Shown in the Scriptures

As recorded in Matthew 28, Jesus commanded His followers to make disciples. As told in the beginning of Acts, the Holy Spirit was poured out upon the followers of Jesus, and they began to form the Church. The Church is built on Christians meeting in different venues, whether in their homes, streets, or by the temple courtyard (see Acts 2:42–47). It is through these small groups that new initiates were made welcome and disciples were formed. This was how the Christian faith grew throughout the world during the first few centuries after Jesus's death and ascension.

> *It is through these small groups that new initiates were made welcome and disciples were formed.*

The function of small groups was discipleship, which included direct and active involvement of all members; direct hands-on training and living together cannot be done in a mass setting. These small groups consisted of gathering for the purposes of study, fellowship, eating together, and prayer (Acts 2:42).

We can also see that the apostles did not take the responsibility of managing small groups lightly. Eventually, the management of these groups became so vast that they decided to pass this administrative function (maintenance of existing disciples) to others so that they could focus on reaching more people (making new disciples; Acts 6:1–7).[31] Jesus's command to make new disciples was the key focus of His followers. Such was the understanding and key message of the Great Commission. The church operated and attracted people through discipleship. Their focus was on love for one another. Our modern-day methods of going out to supermarkets to ask people to join our church was not the focus.

To be inclusive, members of small groups demonstrated the power of the Holy Spirit in the streets as the Lord directed (Acts 3:4–7; Acts 6:8). This, too, can be viewed as an aspect of evangelism, but it is one that is derived by discipleship. God can certainly direct any believer to show His glory this way, but one must be in a close relationship with God to be able to hear His guidance to bring this about. True miracles and healings are dependent on that foundation of love, and that is found in small-group discipleship. Making disciples through small groups was how the Great Commission was practiced as the first churches were formed.

The True Gospel Message That Jesus and His Disciples Taught

The gospel message has evolved over the centuries. Biblically, Jesus taught the gospel message in a familiar verse:

> *For this is how God loved the world: He gave his one and only Son, so that everyone who believes in him will not perish but have eternal life*
>
> John 3:16

This message can also be seen in Ephesians 2:1–10, where the passage beautifully tells us of our situation before Christ (vv. 1–3), the turn that God has made for us (v. 4), and the result (vv. 5–10). The gospel message can be summarized in two words in this passage: ὁ δὲ θεὸς (ho de Theos): *but God*.[32] Though we were doomed to death, God saves us by His grace and by His gift alone. It is not because of what we have done or because we have deserved it, but only because God has provided a way (vv. 8–9). He saves us so that we can fulfill God's original plans that He has designed for each of us (v. 10), which refers to great preordained destinies of individuals or of the collective Church.

Going back to the advent of the Church after Jesus's resurrection (Acts 1–6), the richness of relationships between people were clearly visible. People gave to one another, studied, prayed, and shared lives together (Acts 2:42–47). This kind of living is supported by Jesus's teaching to care for others, because that action is to care for God (Matthew 25:40, 45). The ability of people to relate to one another shows that the believers cared about their relationship with God.

> *The ability of people to relate with one another shows that the believers cared about their relationship with God.*

How can people have a deep relationship with God? They can do so by the grace of God (Romans 3:27; Ephesians 2:1–10), where through Jesus's death and faith in what He has done (Romans 3:25–26), they will receive a transformed heart with the Spirit of God in them so that they will be able to follow and connect with the heart of God

> *It is through personal and deep fellowship with one another while seeking God together that the Church grew in numbers and in hearts.*

(Ezekiel 36:26–27). This is the gospel message. It is through personal and deep fellowship with one another while seeking God together that the Church grew in numbers and in hearts.

Unfortunately, this good message has been distorted over time, and the misunderstanding seems to be no different today than during Jesus's day. At the time of Jesus's life on earth, He criticized the so-called believers, particularly the Pharisees and Sadducees, for their lack of true understanding of the Father's heart. The Pharisees, the religious leaders of Jesus's day, taught others to follow the perfect law, but Jesus came and taught that there is no one who can meet that perfect law (Romans 3:23; Romans 8:30–32). For that reason, God Himself had to initiate and take care of this problem of sin so that His people could again draw close to Him. Let us examine how this gospel message has been distorted over time.

The Great Commission as Shown in the First Millennium

> In the beginning the church was a fellowship of men and women centering on the living Christ. Then the church moved to Greece, where it became a philosophy. Then it moved to Rome, where it became an institution. Next it moved to Europe where it became a culture, and, finally, it moved to America where it became an enterprise.[33]

The above quote may sound like a parody, but it contains the sad truth that what Jesus taught has turned into some kind of cultural trend and is no longer about having a rich relationship with God.

A major shift occurred around AD 325, and the focus of Christians toward the Great Commission began to be less about discipleship. This shift changed how the Church operated. Constantine, the Roman emperor from AD 306 to AD 337, created an official separation between clergy and laity at the Council of Nicaea, nationalizing Christianity as the official religion of Rome.[34]

Prior to the nationalization of the Christian religion, Christians gathered together and shared lives with one another. They practiced prayers, good deeds, fasting, and giving to the poor together.[35] However, Christians were now defined with specific roles. This meant that certain people could disciple others, whereas originally *all Christians were expected to make disciples.* The apprenticeship of believers was no longer one-on-one or one with a few, but it took place in large groups because of the separation of title. It became the clergy's responsibility to lead and hear from God, whereas the "laity" were to simply follow their guidance.

This was also compounded by most of society being uneducated and illiterate. In Jesus's times, a blind man, perhaps uneducated, could testify that he had been unable to see, but then was able to see after Jesus healed him. As a result of such sharing, people who were in similar situations were able to hear and experience God. However, this kind of testimony, along with the ability to disciple others who were in similar situations, was effectively eliminated by this divide, and the laity was to become uniform by the specific teachings of the educated clergy.

Those who wanted to go deeper into connecting with God could go study to become clergy, but their teachings and learnings would become uniform due to formalization and greater hierarchy within the clergy. This led to less dependence on the Holy Spirit's guidance, which led to people simply following rules defined by the church.

> *This led to less dependence on the Holy Spirit's guidance, which led to people simply following rules defined by the church.*

Before going further, please stop and consider how we do church today. When we think of doing church, we often think in terms of scheduled times of congregational worship. It is often one educated and dedicated leader who speaks to us unilaterally. The events of the service are all pre-planned, including the songs to be sung and the Bible verses to be read. This is what the fourth century brought about. This was not how the Early Church operated. This is not to say that what we are doing today is wrong, but as children of God, let us recognize that what we know today, and perhaps have been accustomed to since youth, may be faulty. Let us not rely on the trends, the culture, or the religious laws that we are accustomed to, but let us place our trust in God's Word alone.

While this division of clergy and laity was occurring, there were some Christians who wanted to go deeper and beyond the cultural limitation. This led to asceticism, where those desiring to have a deeper

> *People in those days recognized themselves as followers of Jesus as long as they attended the church service and listened to an educated, dedicated leader each week.*

union with God would find solitude away from society in monasteries.[36] They would be secluded from the rest of society to practice being a disciple of Jesus. This, too, is not a picture of discipleship that Jesus taught. Being isolated is not a call of Jesus, and neither is being away from the world. Jesus lived and walked among sinners. Asceticism, too, has removed the discipleship that Jesus commanded. The Great Commission for all believers to make disciples had effectively ended as a result of the Council of Nicaea and asceticism. However, people in those days recognized themselves as followers of Jesus as long as they attended the church service and listened to an educated, dedicated leader each week.

How the Gospel Was Understood until the Protestant Reformation

By AD 325, the Church was becoming more developed and formal, and Rome was gaining greater importance. Along the way, the Church taught that one could be forgiven and secure eternal life in heaven by following their laws and rules. Popes and bishops claimed the authority to tell the layperson if and how their sins could be forgiven. In fact, the bishops had to welcome the "penitents" (sinners) into the community of the Church by reconciling them with the Church. Anyone who had not been reconciled would not be able to take part in the eucharistic communion.[37] Penance laws were established, and the people had to confess their sins to the bishops and follow specific practices that were required of them in order to have their sins absolved—practices such as saying specific prayers, fasting, and taking part with catechumens until their sins were declared forgiven.[38]

In about the sixth and seventh centuries, "penitentials" were compiled. Penitentials were collections of notes from priests who had assigned penance for various confessions, both small and great. As told in these notes, confessors were able to pay for certain offenses or perform special rites a certain number of times or over a specific period of time.[39] Penitentials were standards, like law books, that prescribed the penalty, or acts to be performed, for specific sins.

> *Penitentials were standards, like law books, that prescribed the penalty, or acts to be performed, for specific sins.*

The standardization of penances led to teaching that the penance needed to be repeated according to the number of times the sin was committed.[40] This kind of penance was also called the

> *Salvation was now received through works. Additional works would forgive people of more sins, sometimes even future sins.*

"tariff penance."[41] Over the years, the severity of the acts required for the penance was reduced to pious donations, pilgrimages, and similar meritorious works.[42] In other words, salvation was now received through works. Additional works would forgive people of more sins, sometimes even future sins—a model that Jesus and His disciples did not teach.

In the eleventh century, the concept of purgatory became more widely taught and accepted. Purgatory is supposed to be an intermediate place where the dead would go if they were not perfected enough to enter heaven, but not sinful enough to enter hell. This is the place where such souls would go to be refined by the fire to be perfected.[43] The sins that do not lead to eternal damnation but still need to be purified are called the "temporal sins."[44] Depending on the extent of the sins needing to be purified, the length or severity of the purification could be greater or less. The possibility of the existence of purgatory had been considered because of the Jewish teaching regarding *Gehinnom*.[45] The popularization of purgatory in this era led to a special kind of penance called indulgences.

Indulgences are a special pardon provided by the *power of the Catholic Church*, therefore owned by bishops and popes, that could reduce the amount of suffering that the person would face in purgatory.[46] Though indulgences were initially taught to be only for temporal sins, the system of indulgences became so abused over time that it was claimed that certain indulgences were said to provide salvation. For a higher cost, forgiveness for greater sins that would require longer and more severe penance would be granted.[47]

The Crusades are one example of this—where Pope Urban II took this law of penance further and declared absolute forgiveness of sins, regardless of the seriousness of the sins, for those who participated in the war against the infidels.[48] This meant that one's devotion or faith in Christ no longer mattered, but eternal salvation would be granted simply for taking part in the war.

> *One's devotion or faith in Christ no longer mattered, but eternal salvation would be granted simply for taking part in the war.*

Other kinds of indulgences included getting a deceased loved one out of purgatory for a fee. They also had future investments, just as we have IRAs today, where people can save up for forgiveness of their future sins.[49]

In the late medieval times, between the thirteenth and sixteenth centuries, penance became more of a scoring board where believers would negotiate with the Church to receive credit when they performed certain menial tasks. Examples of these "tasks" would be saying certain prayers, performing acts of devotion, attending places of worship or other kinds of benevolent gatherings, going on pilgrimages, putting on performances and processions, visiting relics, giving charitable donations, and raising money for a good cause.[50]

> *Believers would negotiate with the Church to receive credit when they performed certain menial tasks.*

Professional quaestores ("pardoners") were hired by the Church to collect money for specific projects for the Church. These "pardoners" often exceeded official Church

> *Salvation was now understood as a combination of works and something the wealthy can secure.*

doctrine and promised rewards such as eternal salvation in return for an exorbitant amount of money. The church flourished financially as a result during this age.[51] The Rouen Cathedral is known as the "Butter Tower" because it was built by the funds raised by selling indulgences.[52] Salvation was now understood as a combination of works and something the wealthy can secure.

It was at this time, around the year 1517, that a priest named Martin Luther got enraged at the teaching that salvation could be bought or worked out. His review of the Scriptures showed that salvation is by faith alone because of God's grace. It is not our work that provides salvation. The Protestant Reformation involved separation from the Catholic Church, no longer relying on decisions by the Catholic Church, but going directly to God in faith alone.[53]

The view of salvation adhered to by the Protestants who followed Martin Luther and John Calvin, including the Methodist and Christian and Missionary Alliance groups, are explained in the "Five Solas," which state that salvation is attained by grace alone (*Sola Gratia*), in Christ alone (*Sola Christus*), through faith alone (*Sola Fide*), for the glory of God alone (*Sola Deo Gloria*), and as told in the Scriptures alone (*Sola Scriptura*).[54]

The Great Commission in the Second Millennium

Until the Protestant Reformation, the Catholic Church[55] was the single Christian church that dictated what it meant to be a follower of Christ for more than a millennium. They were led by people who were educated to teach the same methodology and teachings. Their leaders also initiated decisions regarding penance and crusades that turned

> *The culture led people to follow man-made laws again.*

following Christ into further sets of rules one had to follow to become a Christian and have eternal life.[56] Note the irony in this: Jesus came to free people from blindly following laws in order to have His people love and follow God directly (see Matthew 5; Romans 2:17–29; 3:10–12; 8:30–32, etc.), but the culture led people to follow man-made laws again.

In the sixteenth century, Martin Luther challenged the Catholic Church, stating that deeds are not the way to receive salvation, but rather it is by faith and a gift of God, as written in the Scriptures. In 1517, he presented the Ninety-Five Theses, a set of ninety-five points or teachings of the Catholic Church that he felt were not biblical.[57] Luther was eventually excommunicated and was considered an outlaw by the emperor. He translated the Bible into German,[58] the common language of the people of Germany in his day, from Latin, which was used by the Catholic Church and could only be read by specially educated clergymen. The Bible could now be read by the laity to understand the message without the interpretation of the clergy.

However, the Catholic Church believed that the power of interpreting Scripture belonged to the clergy of the Catholic Church. As a result, many people who read the Bible and came to a conclusion other than the official Roman Catholic teaching were excommunicated and killed.[59]

For a thousand years, the Roman Catholic Church had taught that their way of worshipping and communicating with God was the right way. Under the direction of the pope, people spent their life savings for penance that promised them eternal life, and many joined a "holy war," believing that all their past sins would be forgiven. Knowing the Scriptures today, it might be easy for us to point out their faults; however, most Christians back then could not see that what they were doing was faulty. Some people who tried to tell others about the truth of God's Word were ignored and even killed (this seems to be how the prophets of God were treated in the Old Testament).

Even today, we may be facing the same trouble, and many of us, too, may be too blind to see what is wrong, while some who try to bring reform may be ignored, ridiculed, or even killed. This is why it is most important for followers of Jesus to be able to hear His voice correctly. One way to confirm His voice is in a small group of people who love one another and together love God.

> *Even today, we may be facing the same trouble. . . . This is why it is most important for followers of Jesus to be able to hear His voice correctly.*

State of the Great Commission Today

Fast forward to the twentieth and twenty-first centuries, and we see that the members of the clergy are still viewed as people who are to interpret the Bible and do the work of God, while the laity come to worship services and listen to the messages as interpreted by the clergy. This is not in accordance with the Great Commission that Jesus taught.

Through the era of Enlightenment and beyond, education in the sciences became the mark of individual greatness.[60] As a result, theology has come to be viewed as another science.[61] Though there might be benefits of such focused study about God, the understanding of God has become purely educational and academic for much of the clergy. It is no longer about a relationship with God, but is just another certification or profession that members could put on a wall.

> *Understanding of God has become purely educational and academic for much of the clergy. It is no longer about a relationship with God.*

The teachings of the clergy have become very logical and centered toward the natural. The belief in supernatural miracles and healings from God are heavily discounted, if not eliminated completely.[62] Discipleship for individuals and the few are not emphasized, but rather learning from the pulpit has become the norm.[63]

Ministry also becomes less of a calling from God, and is viewed as a job like any other profession.[64] Because of the Industrial Age, people are trained to become efficient in one specific area with the consideration that such efficiencies maximize profits. The concept of the assembly line applies here: a person would be assigned a specific task that is simply repeated, and then the item is passed on to another worker to mass-produce products in the shortest amount of time.[65]

Unlike in previous centuries when prominent figures were multi-talented, an educated person today is one who is able to do one thing well. Such people today may be financial accountants, physicists, or medical doctors, but not all three.

Educational systems, including universities, encourage this by enabling students to select a major, obtain a specialized degree, and work in that field. The path to ordination is no different: a student must enter a seminary (a university for theology), obtain a degree, and then be ordained. There are employment and salary sites that list "pastor" no differently than "structural engineer."[66, 67]

Many laypeople living under the same influence see clergy as a vocation no different than their own vocation as an engineer, architect, or business owner.

> *Many churchgoers believe they are Christians as they focus on and do well in their vocations.*

As a result, many churchgoers believe that their Christian role is only to focus on and do well in their vocations, while they believe that the work of God, including living out the Great Commission, is to be done by the clergy. Many so-called Christians today believe they are Christians because they attend one or more church services each week. Some so-called believers do not feel that church is even needed for them since they can *educationally* learn on their own from the many resources available to them, including books and the internet.[68] This is far from the vision of the Church shown in the Scriptures (see Ephesians 4) and the true Christian faith.[69] Being a disciple of Jesus means living a lifestyle with others in community.

Relationship with God has always been the primary calling since the time of creation (see Genesis 1), and Jesus came to break the cycle of the law of sin

> *Being a disciple of Jesus means living a lifestyle with others in community.*

and death and bring us back to God (Matthew 27:51; Romans 5:1–2; Romans 8:1–2). However, two millennia have passed since Jesus has paved a way for us to reconnect with God, but today's state of

Christianity seems to be following the methods that the world teaches instead of going back to what Jesus taught.

Many churches now view discipleship as having large groups of people come and listen to sermons. People are taught biblical knowledge to increase head knowledge, although heart knowledge is what God longs for (1 Samuel 16:7; Jeremiah 17:10; John 4:24).

Perhaps even our modern-day focus on mass worship was not prescribed by God. Consider other aspects of modern-day worship that may be man-made or formed through marred history: sermons, benedictions, baptisms, the Lord's Supper, and prayers for miracles and healing *solely to be given and administered by ordained pastors.* Even the concept of a sermon to be prepared only by someone who is educated may not stand to be biblical. God used regular people like fishermen to speak boldly to transform many lives. Perhaps it should be *all Christians* who should practice these roles, especially in the midst of others they love, in their small groups.

Transformation from the head to the heart can only be done through focusing back on discipleship. Small groups, as envisioned from the book of Acts, and personal apprenticeship through relationships are the keys to turning back to God. As the people of God walk with Him together, they will experience healings, miracles, raising of the dead, and life transformations. Kevin Watson puts this beautifully:

> Discipleship, however, is about a way of life, not only the life of the mind. Disciples follow Jesus. They are sent out in ministry by Jesus. They heal the sick. They feed the poor. They tell people about Jesus and what He has done.[70]

How can we restore this broken theology? Would we say that professors and theologians today are doing wrong? We must recognize that we live in this fallen world and that our theology might be distorted. Then we can come to God together, asking Him to restore our minds to see what He is doing—and then join in with Him. This is the path to revival and experiencing the heart of God.

John Wesley's Method of Discipleship—Class Meetings

John Wesley is the founder of the Methodist denomination. He was raised in an Anglican family, he was a scholar who received his education from Oxford, and he was a failed pastor at one point in his life.[71] His experiences, especially regarding the Moravians and his eventual encounter with God, is what the people whom God is nudging need today.

Even though Wesley was an ordained pastor, after spending much time with the Moravians, he realized that *he was lacking saving faith*. He had been trying to live a good moral life as he understood from his studying, but he felt he could not attain it. He then had an experience that he shared in his journal on May 24, 1738:

> In the evening, I went very unwillingly to a society in Aldersgate Street, where one was reading Luther's preface to the Epistle to the Romans. About a quarter before nine, while he was describing the change which God works in the heart through faith in Christ, I felt my heart strangely warmed. I felt I did trust in Christ, Christ alone for salvation, and an assurance was given me that he had taken away my sins, even mine, and saved me from the law of sin and death.[72]

Wesley met God.[73] He recognized that it is not through knowledge or one's willingness to live a good life, but it is a gift from God that only He is able to give. He then began to expand on drawing close to God by forming small groups, which he called *classes*.[74]

Classes met "weekly to pray, read the Bible, discuss their spiritual lives, and to collect money for charity."[75] Wesley recognized that a relationship with God was the foremost calling, and therefore, the primary question in these meetings was "How is it with your soul [spirit]?"[76] This essentially asked, "How goes your relationship with God? How is your mind in your day-to-day living in your focus with God? How is God impelling your spirit today?" These questions help Christians to remain focused on their primary goal of living in a relationship with God.[77] This accountability in class meetings gave them another name by which they were frequently called: "Watching over one another in love."[78, 79]

The dramatic change that is seen in these small groups is that each member is called to be accountable in how they are living.[80] As opposed to modern-day services attended by large congregations and Bible studies performed in school-like environments where people are told to absorb what one individual has prepared, each individual is given the helm to share about their current experience and receive feedback from others that can help them learn, encourage them, and ultimately, help them continue to grow in their life of faith.[81]

Some practical considerations of small groups were the number of people, the formation of groups, and the contents of the meeting. Classes

> *Class meetings centered on the central question: "How is it with your soul?"*

had between seven and twelve members, both men and women. Women, as well as men, could lead classes. The classes formed were based on location; neighbors regularly met together. Finally, class meetings centered on the central question: "How is it with your soul?"[82] The effect of the meeting is worded beautifully by Kevin Watson:

The phrase that best captures what the Methodists believed was so important about the class meeting was "watching over one another in love." Early Methodists were asked to invite others into their lives and to be willing to enter deeply into the lives of other people so that together they would grow in grace. They were committed to the idea that the Christian life is a journey of growth in grace, or sanctification. And they believed that they needed one another in order to persevere on this journey. And so, in the early Methodist class meeting, people would gather together, someone would open the meeting with prayer, the group would often sing a song or two, and then the class leader would start by answering the question, "How does your soul prosper?" After participants answered the question, the leader would turn to someone else in the group and ask that individual the same question. The class leader or someone else might occasionally respond to the person's answer by asking another question, offering encouragement, and sometimes giving advice. The basic pattern of the meeting was that simple. People were essentially giving testimony to their experience of God over the past week. And God seems to have used this, as the testimony of others was frequently contagious. People often experienced conversion simply through participating in a class meeting![83]

Since growing in relationship with God was the most important aspect of Wesley's organization, people were removed from church membership if they missed a certain number of meetings:

> What shall we do with those members of society, who wilfully [sic] and repeatedly neglect to meet their class? Answ. 1. Let the elder, deacon, or one of the preachers, visit them, whenever it is practicable, and explain to them the consequence if they continue to

> neglect, viz. Exclusion. 2. If they do not amend, let him who has the charge of the circuit exclude them in the society; shewing that they are laid aside for a breach of our rules of discipline and not for immoral conduct.[84]

Class meetings were the crux of the explosive growth of Methodism, but over time this has declined. Watson explains that this may be due to the development of Sunday schools in the nineteenth century, when, as mentioned in prior paragraphs, education prepared by educated individuals took greater priority over personal interaction and accountability.[85] Additionally, Watson also attributes the decline to the Industrial Age, when lower, middle, and upper classes began to form. Due to the disparities of social classes, people felt more uncomfortable discussing the activities of their daily lives to another person in a different social class. This also led the upper class, or the perceived experts, to teach in a Sunday school manner.[86] This process eventually made class meetings in Methodist churches nearly extinct today:

> Unfortunately, by the beginning of the twentieth century, the class meeting was almost entirely extinct in America. It was occasionally referred to by historians, but it was far easier to find an early Methodist class-meeting ticket than a group of Methodists who were actually meeting together as a class meeting. Instead of talking to each other about their experience of God and their pursuit of holiness, Methodists were talking to each other about much more general and abstract ideas that were increasingly difficult to connect to the intimate and mundane details of their lives. The class meeting had become an archaeological relic of our better days and instead of being a way of life, people began to view their Christian identity as one of a number of hobbies they

might develop or work on when it was either convenient or served to make life a little bit better.[87]

Watson gives three reasons why class meetings should be reinstated in today's Methodist churches:

- The class meeting joins people together in small groups so they are not lost in church.[88]

- The format of the class meeting draws attention every week to the reality that the Christian life is not static.[89]

- Answering the question, "How is it with your soul?" or "How is your life in God?" every week helps to keep "the main thing the main thing."[90]

This is not just needed in Methodist churches, but in all churches. All Christians need to revert back to the model of discipleship that was modeled by Jesus's disciples and was taught by Jesus during His life on earth.

Small-Group Reflections

1. How does your current practice of worship and discipleship match up with what is prescribed in the Scriptures?

2. What do you believe to be your great calling of God? How can you ensure that it is purely from God and is not tainted by the cultural norms and trends?

Chapter Five

Effective Strategies for Evangelism

Culture is religion externalized.

—Henry R. Van Til

There is a trend in the modern-day Church for laypersons to attend local church services simply to retain their desire to be referred to as Christians. Most certainly, no Christian would state this blatantly; however, with the advances from industrialism, young people tend to think of their individual jobs as their sole vocation from God. Sadly, even some pastors see their role as being just a job. The rationale is that as they do well in their vocation, or their job, God will delight in this and bless them. They want to be Christians as they focus on their individual lives first.

This kind of thinking is a result of a Westernized mindset of individualism that has deteriorated many churches today. So-called "Christians" do not place the kingdom of God first, and they are no different from not-yet-Christians as they focus on living the best life they can live, with the tacit thinking that this is what God desires from them.

Additionally, since Christians are no different from the people whose lives are filled with busyness and distractions, Christians are not available to help or guide people when they are crying out

> *So-called "Christians" do not place the kingdom of God first, and they are no different from not-yet-Christians as they focus on living the best life they can live, with the tacit thinking that this is what God desires from them.*

for help and seeking God. Many local churches are also struggling financially, as fewer people are interested in partaking in worship services; as a result, some churches have turned away from the Great Commission and are focusing on *pleasing the current members*. In short, this means that many local churches are no longer missional and many Christians are not involved in the Great Commission. Many Christians actually believe that the Great Commission is only for those who hold the role of pastor, and pastors are often busy.

In this chapter, Jesus's call to discipleship will be reviewed as a preface to great historical movements that led the Church toward discipleship, including that of the development of sodalities. This requires contextualization and sharing lives with people whom God made similar to us in experience and pursuits. Finally, a section is dedicated to a special kind of sodality that gathers like-minded people. Business ownership can allow entry anywhere in the world and can allow business owners to dwell among people who do not know Jesus; this is what the apostle Paul did as he sold tents for a living.

This chapter briefly touches historical events that have brought us to where we are today. However, our history is not yet complete, and it remains for Christians to respond to and complete the call.

Jesus's Call to Make Disciples

Every Christian is a missionary. The Great Commission that Jesus left His disciples before leaving earth is the calling that all followers of Christ must fulfill.

> *Every Christian is a missionary.*

The Great Commission in Matthew 28:19–20 demands that His followers make disciples by going, baptizing, and teaching.

This is consistent with how Jesus lived during His time on earth. Scripture tells us that Jesus came to earth to show us a model of how to live (Matthew 6:9; Hebrews 12:1–3; 1 Peter 2:21). Jesus discipled others through small groups.

His small group stayed close to Him for a period of three years. The close relationship the disciples had with Jesus is very different from the mentorship and coaching of today's modern business culture. Especially in many churches today, it is normal for the members to only see each other once a week. There is no accountability, no prayer for one another, and ultimately, no growth. In a culture where individualism is encouraged, this is the norm; however, this is contrary to the Bible and is not suitable for Jesus's followers.

Jesus had many disciples who followed Him in His daily activities (see Luke 6:12–13; John 6:60–70). However, He was most available to the twelve. Then He spent more of His time with three—Peter, James, and John. Jesus did not give lectures once a week for His "students" to take notes on what He prepared; instead, Jesus lived among them. This kind of discipleship that Jesus lived out is what He calls all believers to do—live lives with other believers.

The concept of dating often seems like a pitch to show one's good side to another person for a short duration. This concept extends to interviews, teachings (in school, church, etc.), and now even online with social media. Real lives are hidden, and people are expected to show only positive sides of their lives while keeping other aspects of their lives to themselves. Since people recognize that they cannot live up to the perfection others outwardly show, they go into hiding. They are filled with weariness, depression, and stress—and this is the state of the individualistic society today.

> *Since people recognize that they cannot live up to the perfection others outwardly show, they go into hiding. They are filled with weariness, depression, and stress—and this is the state of the individualistic society today.*

The Church is not called to be individualistic. We are called to be a community of believers (Acts 2:42–47). This is exactly how the apostles carried out Jesus's command after He arose from the dead and sent them the Holy Spirit. They gathered in homes (v. 46) and shared lives together. Their ability to be transparent enabled them to study the apostle's teaching together and to have fellowship, eat together, and ultimately pray for one another (v. 42).

> *Their ability to be transparent enabled them to study the apostle's teaching together and to have fellowship, eat together, and ultimately pray for one another.*

Evangelism occurs in a community of love, and that is the directive of the Great Commission. It is through our modeling the life of Jesus, whose life was transparent to the few. This often seems very countercultural to many people, especially the people of the Western world. Ralph Winter puts it this way:

Israel tried to be blessed without trying very hard to be a blessing. However, let's be careful: the average citizen of Israel was no more oblivious to the second part of Genesis 12:1–3 than the average Christian today is oblivious to the Great Commission! . . . Thus, how many times in the average church today is the Great Commission mentioned? Even less often than it comes up in the Old Testament![91]

Therefore, the proposal for change in the Church today is that *all Christians around the world should be actively engaged in reaching the unreached through involvement in small groups.* Can this be done? That is what I desire to see.

Passionate Prayer Meetings in Small Groups That Changed the World

When we look back in history, we can clearly see that great things happened because of small groups and their powerful prayer meetings. As many Christian historians know, the Protestant Reformation that developed between the sixteenth and seventeenth centuries was the beginning of the return of individuals studying and searching the Scriptures more deeply to identify what God truly desires from His people, as opposed to blindly following the instructions and practices of the Catholic Church.

> *When we look back in history, we can clearly see that great things happened because of small groups and their powerful prayer meetings.*

In the seventeenth century, some English Reformed Protestants sought to be "purified" from the Catholic practices they felt were "corrupt." They did not like being ruled by a hierarchy of priests, and they "wanted a church with well-trained pastors who would expound the Scriptures faithfully, leading to a church and nation of men and women who were converted and reflected that reality in private and public life."[92] Calling themselves Puritans, they also advocated a greater role for laymen in governing the Church, and they advocated small-group meetings called "conventicles" for Bible study and fellowship.

Puritans were eventually expelled from England and settled in Massachusetts. They evangelized the Algonquin Indians and translated the Bible into their language. Unfortunately, Puritanism did not survive long due to persecution; however, Pietism, another great movement, soon followed.

Influenced by Puritanism, Philipp Spener and some others felt that government influence was a problem that hindered spiritual growth. Seeking small groups for personal growth, Spener formed a "church within a church," also known as a small group. Though pastoral training and preparations were also considered, he placed much focus on lay ministries. During mission journeys, he encouraged better catechetical instruction for the youth and established schools for the poor. This was the beginning of the Pietist movement, which influenced other great movements, including that of the Methodists and the Moravians. Paul Pierson states the importance of small groups in this movement:

> The primary emphases in the movement were the need for personal conversion, the desire to live an authentic Christian life in the midst of a nominally Christian culture, the personal study of Scripture, koinonia, and group prayer. Pietism, like Puritanism, encouraged the laity to read the Bible, finding in it God's word to each person, as well as doctrine for the theologians. . . . The movement developed a strong sense of mission, both within its own society and beyond it to Asia.[93]

It is evident that early movements following the Protestant Reformation recognized the importance of small groups for spiritual growth. In order to grow in intimacy with God, small groups of people dedicated to studying Scripture, praying together, and living out authentic Christian lives were necessary.

> *In order to grow in intimacy with God, small groups of people dedicated to studying Scripture, praying together, and living out authentic Christian lives were necessary.*

As Pierson describes the new Christian movements, he writes a small side section suggesting how to evaluate a renewal movement. He says that a renewal movement: (1) "rediscovers" a forgotten or neglected aspect of the gospel (a "theological breakthrough"); (2) uses some kind of *small group structure*: a church within the Church, thus keeping a link to the larger Church; (3) is committed to the unity, vitality, and wholeness of the larger Church; (4) is oriented toward mission beyond itself; and (5) is conscious of being a distinct covenant-based community.[94]

These movements provide context for the rise, training, and exercise of new forms of ministry and leadership. These movements are flexible as to the form of ministry, while their members remain in close contact with society—especially the poor. The main key points here are that it includes the involvement of *all* Christians, and it is done through the "church in a church" structure, or *small groups*.

Now on to prayer meetings. Beyond the small-group prayer meetings that were the core of Puritanism and Pietism, focused prayer meetings of young individuals have led to great expansion of

> *God has a great plan, and Christians must pray together (in small groups) to unveil the plan of God so that they can take part in the great move of God.*

Effective Strategies for Evangelism   81

the kingdom of God. As we will see, many great moves of God have begun from small-group prayer meetings. This, too, is the call for Christians today. God has a great plan, and Christians must pray together (in small groups) to unveil the plan of God so that they can take part in the great move of God.

There was a small group of people from the country of Moravia (now part of the Czech Republic), a remnant of the Unitas Fratrum (Unity of the Brethren), who were probably influenced by the medieval Christian spiritual movement of Peter Waldo and his followers, the Waldensians. Their beginnings may have been dim, but the Moravians are known for the beginning of the modern worldwide missionary movement.[95] Their worldwide impact began through a group of boys who prayed together.

Count Nicholaus Ludwig von Zinzendorf was born in 1700. In 1714 (at the age of fourteen), he formed the "Order of the Grain of Mustard Seed." This group was formed with five other boys who were dedicated to pray together. Their purpose was to give witness to the power of Jesus Christ and to join other Christians together in fellowship, to help those who were suffering for their faith, and to carry the gospel of Christ overseas.[96]

In 1722, after having gone through much persecution in their homeland, the Moravians came to the home of Zinzendorf and asked

> *Worldwide missions began through the prayers of Christians gathered in small groups.*

if he could help them. He took them into his home, giving them the opportunity to recover.[97] In 1732, he funded the first two Moravian missionaries, who sailed for St. Thomas. Thus, Moravian missions actually began in the hearts of a group of students. Worldwide missions began through the prayers of Christians gathered in small groups.

The Moravian Church shared key features of Puritanism and Pietism. To them, lay leadership was important. People were chosen as elders and teachers not based on social rank or formal education, but based upon their gifts. Pierson describes their practices this way:

> They followed spiritual disciplines with daily prayer and worship. Each person was part of a small group for mutual encouragement, single men with single men, married women with married women, etc. Marriage choices were regulated; people were told whom to marry. Children were separated from their parents at quite an early age, seeing them only at meals. They were a community separate from the world, with a high level of spiritual discipline, ready to go anywhere to spread the Gospel.[98]

The founder of the Methodist Church, John Wesley, was deeply influenced by the Moravians. However, prior to his meeting with the Moravians, John Wesley, along with his brother Charles, began a small group during their college years to devote themselves to becoming holy. Subsequently, the group became known as the "Holy Club." They spent three hours daily (6:00–9:00 a.m.) praying and reading the Psalms and the New Testament. Beyond this, they "translated their piety into an outreach to the poor, the hungry, and the imprisoned."[99]

Despite his early years seeking God, John Wesley was uncertain of his salvation. He struggled with this even after his ordination while he was a pastor. During this troubled time, he set sail for Savannah, Georgia, and met some Moravians on the ship. There was a terrible storm during the voyage, and the passengers were in a panic. Wesley was surprised to see that the Moravians were at peace as they sang hymns and prayed. They "replied that none of their family are afraid to die," and then asked in turn if John Wesley knew for sure that Jesus had saved him. He did not have that assurance at the time.[100] It was from here that Wesley became enamored by the Moravian practices and eventually met Jesus. His journal entries also show times of healing, power encounters, and other things that some might call charismatic today. Wesley had much influence on the Anglican Church, including the transformed slave trader John Newton, who wrote the song "Amazing Grace."[101]

The Methodist Church was founded on the principles that Wesley learned from the Moravians. It is also important to note that such movements have begun with people in small groups who prayed together and pursued holiness through their priorities and way of living, especially in caring for others, as written in the Scriptures.

William Carey was another missionary who made an impact in the Missio Dei.[102] Carey was a Baptist lay preacher and part-time schoolteacher who repaired shoes. He wrote a book, "An Enquiry into the Obligation of Christians to Use Means for the Conversion of the Heathen," where "using means" was referring to establishing mission societies—structured, committed communities of men (and eventually women) who believed in the call to take the gospel to other areas of the world. The contents of his book were divided into four parts:

1. Explains that the Great Commission was binding on all Christians (this was refuted by many of his contemporaries, who said that God can convert people without our help and that we do not need to take part in this).

2. Tells the history of missions thus far.

3. Provides an estimate of the world's population, adherents to other religious groups, and an estimated number of Christians and churches.

4. Suggests how mission societies/structures should be formed.

The modern Protestant missionary movement began in 1800 with William Carey. His book ultimately influenced many people to form missions organizations or small groups with a mission. Other young people, including Samuel Mills, who formed the Haystack Prayer Meeting and eventually made a great impact in China, were spurred by this book to go to other countries where the gospel had not yet been preached.

In 1804, Carey and his associates formed a "brotherhood" in Serampore, India, sharing their possessions and living in community. Their covenant contained eleven statements of purpose:

1. To set an infinite value on people's souls.
2. To acquaint ourselves with the snares that hold the minds of the people.
3. To abstain from whatever deepens India's prejudice against the gospel.
4. To watch for every chance of doing the people good.
5. To preach "Christ crucified" as the grand means of conversion.
6. To esteem and treat Indians as our equals.
7. To guard and build up "the hosts that may be gathered."
8. To cultivate their spiritual gifts, ever pressing upon them their missionary obligation, since only Indians can win India for Christ.
9. To labor unceasingly in Bible translation.
10. To be instant in the nurture of personal religion.

11. To give ourselves without reserve to the Cause.[103]

Within such small groups, Carey desired personal spiritual growth for the members while achieving the goal of building an indigenous church—one that is established by local and native members, by means of native preachers, and by providing the Scriptures in the native tongue. Carey was unique because he relied on tentmaking strategies, which will be discussed in a later section.

> *The goal of building an indigenous church—one that is established by local and native members.*

It was through prayer meetings of small groups that the world was revolutionized. The fervor of those who attended these meetings influenced many, and Christianity is forever transformed because of their acts today. We must pause here to recognize that the work of God, Missio Dei, is not complete. It belongs to the people of today, including you, the reader, to fulfill His calling. This can be done as Christians gather in small groups with fervor and desire to draw close to Him, which can only lead to prayer. Christians who met in small groups to earnestly pray together have changed the world, and there is yet more to come.

> *The work of God, Missio Dei, is not complete. It belongs to the people of today to fulfill His calling.*

Small-Group Movement Outside the Modern-Church Structures - Modalities and Sodalities

Throughout the history of the Church, growth and revival often occurred outside the institutional Church. For example, when Rome declared Christianity their national religion, hierarchy and administrations were built. There was no reason to evangelize, because just being a resident of Rome meant that they were

Christians. This also meant that people felt they were Christians by following the rules of the Roman Catholic Church, such as attending mass every Sunday. Nominalism abounded (very much like today in Western countries, including the United States). However, some people felt that just following rules did not draw them close to God. This is how monasteries came about. Monastic movements have been monumental in the transformation of the Christian Church, including the Protestant Reformation.

Paul Pierson says this on the subject:

> Historically, we have to recognize that most mission movements have not originated at the center of the institutional Church. Most, if not all [missions], have originated on its periphery. . . . Often a layman or woman had a vision that the Church as a whole did not share: Wycliffe Bible Translators, YWAM, OMF . . .[104]

Ralph D. Winter used the terms "modality" and "sodality" to distinguish between the mainstream church and those fellowships that originated from outside the mainstream church. In his "Two Structures of God's Redemptive Mission," Winter describes modality and sodality. He says that modality is a "structured fellowship in which there is no distinction of sex or age," and he defines sodality as a "structured fellowship in which membership involves an adult second decision beyond modality membership and is limited by either age or sex or marital status."[105]

Winter provides an example in which a town is a modality and a private business is a sodality. One belongs in a certain town, and membership in that town requires very little. On the other hand, to initiate a private business requires a personal decision and dedication to keep it running. Likewise, the Church does not require much for a person to become a member; however, taking on additional pursuits in addition to the activities of the mainstream Church requires personal decision, resolve, and dedication.

Missions were often led by the non-mainstream church. The mainstream church has evolved to be more of a pastorate to care for the already-believing-Christians; that is, they have less missional aspects. Pierson purports that the main church structure has its roles, and the "periphery" plays a major role in encompassing both missions and maintenance of the Church. This means that one cannot claim that the mainstream church is either more important or better than a "periphery" ministry that seeks to support the mainstream church. Both are important for the kingdom of God, and they both make up the universal Church.

> *This means that one cannot claim that the mainstream church is either more important or better than a "periphery" ministry that seeks to support the mainstream church. Both are important for the kingdom of God, and they both make up the universal Church.*

Pierson also suggests rejecting the term "parachurch," as it connotes that mission structures are "something less than the Church."[106] Prayer Tents has accepted this term and has replaced the word "parachurch" with "missional," recognizing its place in the global Church.

When the past hundred years are considered, it is evident that the sodalities, such as Campus Crusade for Christ (now CRU), Navigators, Promise Keepers, and InterVarsity Christian Fellowship, have transformed the modern Christian environment. Some of these sodalities focused on youth so that the youth might have a vision of seeking and doing great things for God. Some focused on sharing the gospel, and others focused on missions around the world. They were so influential that some Christians might think that they were part of the mainstream church; however, they were missional organizations that supported the mainstream church. They were sodalities, and if they did not exist, our mainstream church might not be the same as it is today.

The current call is for all Christians to take part to support the Missio Dei. This can occur in small-group settings, where people come with the intent to grow and draw closer to God. As a result of their meeting together for the sake of knowing God more, prayer and executing God's plans will result.

Small groups within a mainstream church structure may be limiting, as they may be expected to carry out administrative church activities and/or submit to the curriculum laid out by church leadership.

> *Small groups within a mainstream church structure may be limiting, as they may be expected to carry out administrative church activities and/or submit to the curriculum laid out by church leadership.*

However, a fluid small group of people without such limitations, but only their own resolve to pursue God and do the will of God together, can direct themselves as to what needs to be done.

As an example of sodality, one promising small group that exists outside the structure of a local church is CBMC, the *Christian Business Men's Connection*. Businesspeople from around the world meet in their localities with the intention of personal growth in Christ, as well as to devote their marketplace experiences and circumstances to God. Beyond the benefits for these Christian men, they are also able to welcome other businesspeople who may not be Christians to join them as they share their own unique business/personal struggles. As a result of such a relationship-making environment, they have the potential to take the gospel to many people whom the mainstream church may not be able to reach.

CBMC is also unique because it is very focused on who it can reach. It is only for men who own businesses or are professionals.[107] Such sodalities can also exist for other focuses of interest, such as women employees, seniors in retirement, or young musicians.

Small-group movement must occur outside the mainstream church with focuses that can draw Christians to discipleship, while also allowing them to invite not-yet-Christians to dialogue with them over time. Missio Dei exists everywhere Christians may be. That is the reason why focusing on people's interests is important to the small-group movement; this is called contextualization.

> *Small-group movement must occur outside the mainstream church with focuses that can draw Christians to discipleship, while also allowing them to invite not-yet-Christians to dialogue with them over time.*

Contextualization—Understanding People Where They Are and Speaking in a Way They Can Understand

Both failed and successful missions can be found throughout the history of missions. Successful missions involve targeted people coming to know God and desiring to know Him more. Failed missions involve targeted people who were often appalled by God and His people. History shows that missions are successful when missionaries contextualize the environment and culture of the people they desire to reach.

> *History shows that missions are successful when missionaries contextualize the environment and culture of the people they desire to reach.*

Consider the way we do church. Perhaps we are Americans who have grown up in church environments singing songs by Chris

Tomlin and holding weekly Bible studies in addition to Lord's Day worship services. If we were to go to a people who are different from us with the intent of sharing the gospel with them, would we declare that they are not open to God and may even be on the way to hell if they do not follow our traditions?

Truly successful missionaries have willingly stayed with the people they ministered to for a long time, perhaps without saying a word about Jesus. Their intent was to learn the people's culture, language, and everyday way of life. If asked in the first two years if they had borne any fruit, they might not be able to provide a desirable answer; however, in the long run, they are the ones who bear lasting fruit for the people in that region.

Growing up in a Korean church, I thought it was normal for all churches to have early morning prayers. When Korean pastors preach about why Christians should pray in the morning in the church, they generally point to Mark 1:35, where Jesus prayed early in the morning. Does that mean that people in non-Korean churches who do not gather together to pray every morning are in the wrong, and perhaps are on their way to hell? Of course, the answer is no; but the success of the Korean church came about because of the missionaries who faithfully adapted to the Korean culture back in the late 1800s.

Morning prayers in Korean churches have attributed to significant revivals that resulted in the conversion of much of the nation of Korea to Christ even though Jesus was not known just a century ago. Surprisingly, the largest church in the world today is in Korea.[108] So because of the fruit shown here, should churches in other countries pray in the morning? The answer again is no. It worked for the Koreans because of their context, but it might not work for another culture.

Prior to missionary movements in Korea, Korea was a country that worshipped ancestors. The Koreans were heavily influenced by

> *Instead of rebuking their practices, the missionaries redeemed this cultural habit by enabling new Christians to continue to do the same activity, but to instead pray to the true God who deserves the worship.*

Shamanism, Shintoism, and other religions. Christian missionaries went to Korea in the nineteenth century and simply observed the ways of the Korean people instead of telling them how they should live. One of the key activities of many Koreans was to wake up early in the morning to bow and give sacrifices to their ancestors.[109] Instead of rebuking their practices, the missionaries *redeemed* this cultural habit by enabling new Christians to continue to do the same activity, but to instead pray to the true God who deserves the worship. Korea is an example of a successful missionary activity, and this is due to the great missionaries who faithfully learned and adapted to the Korean context.

An example of a failed missionary endeavor is when Christians came to the United States from Europe. They desired to have religious freedom apart from the Catholic Church, and they thought they could teach the locals who were already living there with the good gospel they had.

American Indians valued land and community. Some Christian immigrants from Europe may have had a positive intent to share the gospel, but taking away land that the Indians were one with, and mandating that they worship God exactly as they did, put a roadblock in the Christians' ability to influence them. This pain still exists in their hearts today, and some American churches today send people on missions to help Native Americans, hoping to earn back their trust.

There are many other examples that show that investing time in relationships and getting to know the other party results in fruit in

> *Two main characters who practiced contextualization for the sake of evangelism are right in the Bible, namely Jesus and the apostle Paul.*

evangelism. Two main characters who practiced contextualization for the sake of evangelism are right in the Bible, namely Jesus and the apostle Paul. Jesus had a strange way of teaching. When He spoke to the Jews, He spoke of the law of the Tanakh, the Jewish Scriptures. When He spoke to a woman who was tired of obtaining water day after day in the burning heat, He spoke of the Living Water. When He spoke to the hungry crowds, He fed them.

The apostle Paul was no different. Many instances exist in Acts, but the clearest instance of contextualization is seen in Acts 17. Paul saw the polytheistic state of Athens. Paul had been speaking from his Jewish background as he addressed the Jews. This time around, though, when he addressed the people of Athens, he did not speak that same message. Instead, he spoke to what mattered to them the most—their pride in religion (Acts 17:22). Then, without changing the subject, he pointed to a god in whom they believed and with whom they associated—the "unknown" god. Paul claimed that this unknown god was the true God who is above all other gods. More of Paul's contextualization in pagan countries can be seen in his letter to the Colossians, as well as in some of his other letters.

Contextualization showing success in evangelism is seen throughout Christian history. George G. Hunter tells the story of how Patrick became a successful missionary to the Irish in the sixth century.[110] At a young age, Patrick was taken as a slave to Ireland, which was then a pagan country. While he was there, Patrick came to know the people of Ireland, including their culture and language.

Later, he went back to Britain and became a priest. He then decided to return to Ireland and minister to the Irish (become a missionary). His decision and actions were viewed as unthinkable since the Celtics—the Irish—were known to be barbarians who could not be changed.

Mission leaders at that time embraced two goals of Christian mission: to civilize people and to evangelize—though the priority of those goals was uncertain. They believed that the people must become somewhat civilized in order to understand and accept the Christian faith. It was the same in Roman times and in the time of Patrick. That is, many believed that people must be forced to behave a certain way, and then taught to read and speak Latin, adopt Roman customs, and *do* church.

The Irish were considered barbarians by the Roman church because they simply did not know them. Though Patrick's mission seemed impossible to others, his biggest advantage was that he knew the Irish—their language, culture, issues, and ways.

> *Though Patrick's mission seemed impossible to others, his biggest advantage was that he knew the Irish—their language, culture, issues, and ways.*

Patrick was known for powerful spiritual encounters in the pagan lands that resulted in people coming to faith. He also formed monasteries in the new land that were missional. Ireland was a Christian country by the time he died. Patrick's spiritual descendent, Columba, ministered in Scotland. Gregory the Great and Augustine ministered in the British Isles. Columbanus ministered to the Franks (predecessors of the French), and then went to Italy.[111]

While seeing the spiritual success, British church leaders were offended that Patrick and his bishops spent much of their time with pagans, sinners, and barbarians,

> *Church leaders were offended that Patrick and his bishops spent much of their time with pagans, sinners, and barbarians.*

believing that the role of a bishop was to care for the existing flock. Such poor attitudes may exist in some churches today.[112]

In the seventeenth century, the mission in Japan was not as successful because the missionaries did not make use of familiar Shinto and Buddhist terms. For that reason, Japan shut the missionaries out by persecution and martyrdom and did not allow them to enter again for two centuries.[113]

There was also a movement by Robert de Nobili to win over the Brahmin caste in India. He became one himself—a Christian Brahmin. He dressed as a guru and observed the caste laws and customs. He shared the Christian doctrine as much as possible in Hindu terms. As a result, he was successful in winning over the hearts of many Brahmins.[114]

In the eighteenth century, the Moravian church led a mission to the "most despised and neglected people."[115] They were also self-supporting. This not only enabled the missionaries to raise funds as people supported their businesses, but it also allowed them to become intimately connected with their neighbors. Using business for evangelism will be covered in the next section.

Small groups are not only excellent ways for Christians to grow, but they are also excellent ways to welcome new interested believers. Having a common

> *Small groups welcome not-yet-believers who are interested in learning about God, and they can be part of the group without any time-pressure commitment and without anyone trying to force them to believe in God. They can just meet as friends do, asking questions or even asking for prayer as desired.*

interest as a platform for small groups also welcomes not-yet-believers who are interested in learning about God, and they can be part of the group without any time-pressure commitment and without anyone trying to force them to believe in God. They can just meet as friends do, asking questions or even asking for prayer as desired. They can also simply observe the Christians as they go through their small-group activities—perhaps seeing the love of Jesus that is in their midst—whether they are praying, reading the Bible, or just sharing everyday life.

Use of Business Models to Reach the Less Accessible

Business ownership can be another common-interest platform to gather like-minded people. Such gatherings can be used for evangelism, as described

> *Businesses often support neighborhoods in which they are located. As a result, the owners and employees have a unique method to connect and relate with the locals, especially those whom the local churches may not be able to reach.*

in the above sections. However, business is unique in that it can generate funds to sustain mission work. Additionally, businesses often support neighborhoods in which they are located. As a result, the owners and employees have a unique method to connect and relate with the locals, especially those whom the local churches may not be able to reach.

The apostle Paul was called a tentmaker because he supported himself financially by making tents (Acts 18:3; 20:34). *Tentmaker* is a term that now refers to people dedicated to the work of a pastor (or missionary, evangelist, etc.), yet who also support the marketplace. To some, this might mean that the person must be a pastor in addition to being an employee or an owner of a business. Yet all Christians in the marketplace are tentmakers since they make a living in the secular world while serving Christ.

> *All Christians in the marketplace are tentmakers.*

William Carey both assimilated with people in India and supported himself financially by being a professor of Sanskrit, the language of the locals there, for forty years. He also established the concept of a savings bank to help meet the financial needs of the people. At the same time, he formed mission societies to spread the gospel. In other words, he played a dual role of a businessperson and a missionary.

Tentmaking has several obstacles that can make it challenging. As a tentmaker focuses on building profits and investing funds into his or her own business, there may be opposition from less knowledgeable members of the church who say that one ought to live humbly and be less focused on building wealth. Additionally, friends and family may not know what the tentmakers are doing, and they may even try to persuade them from continuing. Additionally, with societal and educational teachings and influences from people close to them, they might struggle to ensure that their foundation is built upon the Rock and not geared toward the world. While operating a business, one must be certain to live and work with the highest level of ethics to maximize one's influence as a Christian. Managing time between work and ministry is another major challenge.

Patrick Lai lists seven reasons why tentmaking fails:

1. Marriage problems
2. Poor leadership
3. Unrealistic expectations
4. Lack of teamwork
5. Sexual sins
6. Inadequate funding
7. Satan[116]

He additionally states, "Among the top qualities of poor leaders are: indecisiveness, lack of focus, limited vision, unwillingness to sacrifice for their people, mistrust of workers, failure to train up others, and pride."[117]

Stephen Bailey says that business missions can be honest since "whatever Christians do, they do it to the glory of God."[118] He also adds, "but when we embrace the idea of a Christian vocation, we are free to see ourselves as Christian businesspeople. We are in mission because all Christians are to be in mission and to live by the principles of the Kingdom that require Jesus' disciples to care about their neighbors."[119] He then goes on to list some advantages and challenges of tentmakers that are abstracted and translated from the writings of Cyrus Lam:

Advantages of Tentmaking

- Easy to participate

- Multiply manpower (can fill many spots)
- Open closed doors (tentmakers gain access to closed countries)
- Increase channels (different ways of getting in with the gospel)
- Bridge preparation (bridge the gap between community and gospel)
- Economical (self-supporting means more resources are available for the Church to help others)
- Maintain one's profession
- Make a visible impact
- Fulfill roles in missions (not just spiritual, but also sociological and developing needs)

Problems with Tentmaking

- Insufficient training (should get theological training early)
- Living standard is too high (tentmakers should be aware of others they are serving when their living standards are higher)
- Difficult fundraising (cannot support oneself fully due to lack of time with dual roles as missionary and worker, and perhaps the expectations of the public)
- Dual responsibilities
- Lack of fellowship
- Unseen results—follow-ups are in secret, personal work is difficult
- Short-term mentality[120]

Tentmaking is a valuable mentality for a Christian. There are limitations of being a Christian worker, such as a pastor, to reach many people. For example, a not-yet-believing young man who is seeking career growth may not find interest speaking with a pastor who may not directly be able to support him in his goals. Businesspeople are more able to go to many places in the world to build relationships and contextualize with others than the institutionalized church can. This is where the concept of sodality shows strength. Mission agencies, including businesses of tentmakers, are sodalities that can meet the call of the Great Commission that the mainstream church may not be able to meet.

> *Businesspeople are more able to go to many places in the world to build relationships and contextualize with others than the institutionalized church can.*

What this means is that the modality church should encourage people in the marketplace and welcome them to build profits for the kingdom of God. Teach them humility and help those in need, yet share about the benefits the apostle Paul was able to bring by working with his hands and dwelling with people of different cultures to meet them where they are.

As we conclude this section, let us consider the great risks involved in tentmaking that the Church should recognize and help support. Patrick Lai talks of a person who would quit his steady income job to focus on mission work. He would take on the risk of having no pay while he studied language and culture so that he could start a business in another country. He may go to that country knowing that after spending much time and money, the government may decide to close the business altogether for political reasons—reasons beyond his control.

Theology of Contextualization

Grenz and Olson write that anyone who has a certain view about God and asks about life's ultimate questions is a theologian. All people seek the truth about their assumptions and understanding of God, and therefore, everyone is a theologian, even though they might not have the right theology.[121] Theology is simply a human understanding about God.

> *Everyone is a theologian, even though they might not have the right theology.*

Theology became important because, in light of the Scriptures, many incorrect (false) theologies existed, not just as evident today, but even in the times of the Early Church Fathers.[122] Grenz and Olson write that the critical task of a Christian regarding theology is "to examine beliefs and teachings about God, ourselves, and the world in light of Christian sources, especially the primary norm of the Biblical message."[123]

The second critical task is to "set forth the unity and coherence of the Biblical teaching about God, ourselves, and the world in the *context* in which God calls us to be disciples" (emphasis added).[124] They summarize that the theology needed today is that which is "truly scriptural, completely Christian, and totally relevant."[125]

> *The theology needed today is that which is truly scriptural, completely Christian, and totally relevant.*

Relevance refers to contextualization. Grenz and Olson continue, saying that Scripture and heritage (history) are the two main tools of theology, and from those two tools we must derive messages that speak to the context of our present times, locality, and culture.[126]

They also emphasize that the message must be understandable to people and must be kept relevant, speaking to the current problems, longings, and ethos of contemporary culture.

> *The message must be understandable to people and must be kept relevant, speaking to the current problems, longings, and ethos of contemporary culture.*

Also, the message must take seriously contemporary discoveries and insights of various disciplines of human learning, as "all truth is God's truth."[127]

To contextualize theology, Grenz and Olson suggest beginning with the culture instead of with the Bible. They explain that contextualization occurs:

> . . . by observing people around us, listening to their conversations, keeping up with the news, becoming aware of cultural expressions of a deeper spiritual quest, following intellectual developments, and even studying philosophy. We observe and listen so as to discern the questions and concerns of contemporary men and women. Having discovered these, we go back to the Bible for a response. We take our culture with us to the texts. We read the Scriptures asking, "How does the Bible provide answers to the questions people today are raising?"[128]

They state that this is the accurate way as taught by the Scriptures by pointing to Jesus's model of ministry to the Samaritan woman and Nicodemus.

> *Good theology always affects life, which refers to having the ability to touch one's needs and longings.*

They also make the case that good theology always affects life, which refers to having the ability to touch one's needs and longings.[129]

Theology that is contextualized is called local theology. It is a "dynamic interaction among gospel, church, and culture."[130] It is local because that theology works only for people of that specific location and culture. For example, Western theology had been developed for centuries with the thought that it would be usable in other countries, but it turns out to be socially biased.[131] In fact, many popular theologies are local theologies. For example, liberation theology is a local, or contextualized, theology that works for the people in Latin America because of the oppression they experience.[132] The same theology cannot be applied to those in the United States, who generally do not experience the same oppression.

Why do new theologies such as Prosperity Theology, Emerging Church Theology, and Black Theology continue to be developed? It is because contextual questions of the local area could not find answers in traditional or existing theologies. For example, how would one perform the Eucharist when wine is not available in specific regions, or how would someone baptize someone when pouring water on someone's head is a curse of infertility? Traditional theology would not be able to answer these questions, so new theologies are formed.[133]

In order to build contextualized (local) theologies, one must include *all* people. Contextualization is not done by specially trained theologians, nor is it done by church leadership alone; instead, everyone must be included in creating the unified theology.[134] Common problems that people face every day can be answered in light of the gospel through contextualization.

> *Contextualization is not done by specially trained theologians, nor is it done by church leadership alone; instead, everyone must be included in creating the unified theology.*

Effective Strategies for Evangelism   103

Paul uses a "yes, but" strategy in answering the question regarding eating foods offered to pagan gods. He also adopts and redefines key terms that the Corinthians often used, such as "knowledge," "right," "conscience," and "weak." Paul also redefines the well-known *Shema* based on Deuteronomy 6—that there is one God—and reinterprets it Christologically: *But for us, there is one God, the Father, by whom all things were created and for whom we live. And there is one Lord, Jesus Christ, through whom all things were created, and through whom we live* (1 Corinthians 8:6).

Stephen Bevans agrees that contextualizing is not on the "fringes" of theology, but is at the center.[135] He proposes six models of contextual theology: Anthropological, Transcendental, Praxis, Synthetic, Translational, and Countercultural.

- The Anthropological Model is "the preservation of Christian identity while attempting to take culture, social change, and history seriously."[136] In other words, it begins with the focus on the *anthropos*, or human. The Anthropological Model is valuable because "revelation is not essentially a message, but the result of an encounter with God's loving and healing power in the midst of the ordinariness of life."[137] It also starts with where each individual is. However, there is a greater risk of falling into human/cultural romanticism. Examples of the Anthropological Model are Liberation Theology and the Naked Gospel.

- The Transcendental Model is based on the thought that one cannot understand without a complete change of mind. The thinking does not begin from the gospel or from the content of the tradition, but from the people—from the people's own context. The Transcendental Model is contextual theology capturing the experience of the past (Scripture and tradition) and the experience of the present (experience, culture, social location, and social change).[138]

- The Praxis Model is a method of continued improvement that is initiated with a small action. It is circular: it begins with some specific action, and then one reflects on the action and/or the results of that action with the Scriptures, prayer, etc. Then that same action is taken again, but with greater refinement. The Praxis Model is focused on the now (or recent) revelations of God. It can also be called "situational theology." Bevans seems to emphasize this as the best way of doing contextual theology, as he states that the Praxis Model "promises to be one of the most powerful."[139]

- The Synthetic Model refers to the synthesis of all models examined. It attempts to preserve the importance of the gospel message and the heritage of traditional doctrinal formulations while also considering the current contexts. An example would be the theological activities of Jose M. de Mesa. He was a scholarly person holding a Ph.D. who did not lay down any particular theological method; instead, he proposed scholarly methods, but he continued to study the present context using other theological methods.[140]

- The Translational Model begins with understanding the core message of Scripture, and then recommunicating the main message in a meaningful way for the listener. An example of the Translational Model is David Hesselgrave coming up with a new tract for Chinese readers instead of translating the English directly into Chinese (which would have maintained the English cultural understanding). The new tract for the Chinese would be culturally appropriate for the people of the Chinese culture.[141]

- The Countercultural Model is a bit of a misnomer, as it is not opposed to the existing culture. Culture itself is not evil, and the intent would be to be as engaging and relevant as possible; however, the gospel needs to challenge and purify the context if the gospel is to take true root in people's context. Bevans states that this model is the most contextual while retaining faithfulness to the gospel.[142]

Therefore, good theology is contextualized to local, or similar, people, and it is life-transforming theology.[143] That is why it is important to group like-minded, or like-focused, people together to theologize together so they can contextualize in their own contexts. Interest-based small groups will be discussed in the following section.

Correct theology is about living it out and bringing our lives to God together in community just as we are. Osias Segura-Guzman says this about good theology:

> *Correct theology is about living it out and bringing our lives to God together in community just as we are.*

> Good Theology and its application, Christian praxis, has to begin with a community of believers bringing their experiences and struggles to the Scriptures, reflecting on them and purifying that reflection into action, all with the purpose of spiritual growth and social transformation. That should be a local church's task, where a group of people talk to and about God, bringing God into their life struggles, listening to God and to one another, and bringing this reflection into the context in which they live.[144]

Interest-based Small Groups

One way that Christians can fulfill the call of the Great Commission is to form sodalities that are able to contextualize and form potentially long-term relationships with neighbors who are similar to each other. Additionally, Christians can only make disciples if they are disciples themselves—if they are people who are daily growing in Christ together in community. Just as Jesus and His disciples demonstrated, the formation of small groups is the platform for discipleship.

The local church may be less equipped to attract people outside the church because of a predominant religious affiliation. In order to meet the unique needs, desires, and pursuits of individuals, interest-based small groups outside church structures may be needed.

> *In order to meet the unique needs, desires, and pursuits of individuals, interest-based small groups outside church structures may be needed.*

Using the information we have reviewed thus far, here is a usable definition of small groups: *A small group is self-directed and consists of three or more similar Christians in proximity to each other who personally seek to grow closer to Christ and are willing to share their lives together.*

> *A small group is self-directed and consists of three or more similar Christians in proximity to each other who personally seek to grow closer to Christ and are willing to share their lives together.*

When the group's membership reaches about ten, the group should consider dividing in order to keep the groups small. The reason for the absolute necessity of small numbers is to ensure full engagement, involvement, and participation of all small-group members. Additionally, when not-yet-believers partake in the group, they require an atmosphere where they are free to express themselves and ask any questions they may have. A larger group would both intimidate the newcomer and cause the newcomer to think that perhaps he or she should remain quiet and allow others to do all the talking.

As an example of small groups that were successful by focusing on interests, experiences, and similarities, let us go back in time to the nineteenth century. Missionaries of that age were evangelists at heart, spending much time saving souls through relationships and planting churches with similar people. Along the way, specialization in missions began to form.

Medical missions (sometimes referred to as "Angels of Mercy") was a specialty. One example of such a person is Wilfred Grenfell, a missionary doctor to Labrador. Another is John Scudder, a doctor who served in India with his family. He had more children in India, including a daughter, Ida Scudder. Ida built a nursing school for women and raised funds to meet the needs of the ministry. Another example is Carl Becker, who received his medical education in America and became a medical missionary in Africa. One African tribe consisting of Pygmies came to trust the missionaries, overcoming their initial distrust because of the missionaries' ability to treat wounds and care for the hurting.[145] Though each of these respective missions has grown in size over time, small beginnings in small groups enabled the growth.

Other specialties include those focusing on Bible translations, such as the Summer Institute of Linguistics, Wycliffe Bible Translators, and radio operators such as Clarence W. Jones. Aviators formed the Mission Aviation Fellowship (MAF) to help missionaries travel over far distances, especially over swamps filled with deadly diseases and dangerous creatures. Betty Greene, who served with the

Women Airforce Service Pilots during WWII, was one of the founders of MAF. Nate Saint was one of the flyers, and was eventually martyred by Auca tribesmen in 1956.[146]

Though the above are only a few examples of mission-focused groups, it shows that when Christians gather together for common good based on their interests, experiences, and similarities, they can do great things as they serve Christ.

> *When Christians gather together for common good based on their interests, experiences, and similarities, they can do great things as they serve Christ.*

Combining the ability to do great things together, the ability to grow individually as Christians, and the desire to make disciples of people similar to them, small groups can be used mightily by God. As a reminder, great things of God have often been borne from the prayers of small groups. I long to see an explosion of these small groups that would make God's name known by what He would do through them. Local churches should celebrate the differences of individuals and their callings and encourage them to connect with others, even outside their churches, who have similarities.

Reliance on the Holy Spirit to Do Mighty Things through Small Groups

After studying Isaiah 54:2–3, William Carey formulated this famous missionary motto that persists even today: "Expect great things from God; attempt great things for God."[147] Small groups have the ability to jointly expect and attempt great things for God.

> *Small groups have the ability to jointly expect and attempt great things for God.*

In our modern day, especially for the people in Western countries, many people rely on the existing foundations of science. Paul A. Pomerville tells us that the reason why there seems to be such "estrangement of Western Christianity and the Spirit" is because people have shifted to scholasticism and apologetics.[148]

Timothy C. Tennent agrees that Westernized thinking does not recognize that God can heal and bring about miracles. Consumer-driven churches today are following business models in the capitalistic society. The historic Church privatized salvation and has "given the church a mere instrumental role" where we are to "merely look back and tell the world what happened at the cross and the resurrection." However, we must recognize that it did not end there, but that it "continues to unfold in God's ongoing initiatives at Pentecost"[149] and the movement of the Holy Spirit. Paul Pierson states, "The theology of non-Western churches, with rare exceptions, is solidly evangelical. Often they show greater spiritual vitality and evangelistic zeal than the West. In many cases, their prayer life is deeper and they expect God to work with power."[150]

In order for the Western countries to experience revival, Christians need to rely less on the promises of the world—including employment, technology, and money; instead, they need to rely on the Holy Spirit so that every church gathering consists of an explosion of testimonies of what

> *In order for the Western countries to experience revival, Christians need to rely less on the promises of the world—including employment, technology, and money; instead, they need to rely on the Holy Spirit so that every church gathering consists of an explosion of testimonies of what God is doing.*

110   Our Highest Calling

God is doing. Pierson reminds us that relying on the Holy Spirit means being open to going beyond what is safe and normal:

> I do not think God is primarily concerned with creating beautiful, shiny new Christians who never get scratched. That would be like buying a new car and storing it safely in the garage where it will not get dented. I believe that the person who is filled with the Holy Spirit and following His leading will often get bruised and battered. He or she may not always be the kind of person who can get up at every prayer meeting and give a triumphant testimony of how great things are.[151]

Many preachers have spoken about returning to what the first church looked like, and they often point to the second chapter of Acts. However, many forget that this church was formed out of small groups that shared everything together and consisted of members who were hungry for the Word of God, prayer, and fellowship with one another. Pierson says, "The Christian mission remains the same, but our context is very different from that of Zinzendorf, Carey, or Hudson Taylor. That fact calls us to sensitivity to each culture, hard thinking, and openness to the creativity of the Holy Spirit."[152] Through interest-based small groups that are decentralized from the local church and can welcome anyone who is interested in learning about God, I believe God can do mighty things. The Great Commission will be fulfilled in many places around the world, making disciples as Christians themselves also mature in their walk with God.

Effective Strategies for Evangelism

Small-Group Reflections

1. How are you *all things to all people* for the sake of winning them to Christ?

2. Patrick was an effective missionary to the Irish because he knew their culture and language. To whom would you have an effective ministry based on the context God has given you?

3. How do you believe that God has prepared you to fulfill His great calling for your life?

Chapter Six

Our Highest Calling Is Love

"You must love the Lord your God with all your heart, all your soul, and all your mind." This is the first and greatest commandment. A second is equally important: "Love your neighbor as yourself." The entire law and all the demands of the prophets are based on these two commandments.

—Jesus[153]

Love has always been the highest calling; don't substitute it for anything less.

When the public thinks about the concepts of love, relationships, and community, church is not the first thing that comes to mind. That is not good, because these are the highest values of being a follower of Jesus.

Many churches currently speak of having a relationship with God, yet we live in a world where people no longer recognize what having a relationship means. The younger generation (often labeled as Generation Z) has many distractions (social media, games, and other individually directed marketing) that might prevent them from knowing how a relationship works. Their connections with people are usually short and sporadic. The older generations (often labeled Millennial or Generation X/Y) have relationships that are often a combination of being busy

> *When the public thinks about the concepts of love, relationships, and community, church is not the first thing that comes to mind.*

and living out the Facebook-like lifestyle; that is, they portray only the positive aspects of life, having to hold in anything that could put them in a bad light. As a result, their relationships are shallow, having very few examples of strong relationships.

Additionally, busy parents in this generation are unable to have real relationships with their growing children, leading

> *Children (may) consider real relationships to be undependable, noncommittal, and unimportant.*

the next generation to consider relationships as less meaningful. This is also compounded with the still-high divorce rates (around 50 percent) that lead children to consider real relationships to be undependable, noncommittal, and unimportant.

A close relationship with God cannot be achieved when we do not have a framework as to what a relationship looks like. God has given us human

> *We cannot love God without understanding how we should love others.*

parents and human neighbors so that we can understand what a real relationship with God looks like (see Matthew 22:37–40; Matthew 25:31–46). We cannot love God without understanding how we should love others. As we love others, or are able to be in relationship with them, we can love God and be in relationship with Him (see 1 John 4:7–8).

In our modern day, some churches do have small groups, but they often gather for a different reason than why small groups should exist. They may have a mandate to meet once a month, and it is often executed as a business task to check off to show that they have done so. However, small groups are intended to be made up of people who meet together with unrushed time, whether they have things to say or not, whether they are going through good times or the bad, just to connect with and be there for each other.

Additionally, due to the social-media age of relationships, many people do not know what is going on in the lives of other people. Rather, they often remain at the surface level, similar to asking, "How are you doing?" with the response simply being, "I'm fine." It is often no different in church communities.

This is also combined with shallow prayer requests. When asked for prayer requests, many people only provide impersonal requests such as asking others to pray for their friend's sick mother. As Christians, God calls us to great things, and we will have struggles, obstacles, waiting, and the need for God's breakthrough and miracles where we must stand together and encourage one another; yet these are not apparent in small groups that are patterned after our culture today. This is one reason why the Church lacks power and is not known for love, unity, relationships, or community today.

> *As Christians, God calls us to great things, and we will have struggles, obstacles, waiting, and the need for God's breakthrough and miracles where we must stand together and encourage one another.*

What Should a Small Group Look Like?

A true small group is a group of people in relationship with one another, supporting one another to remain in relationship with God together. Through their deep relationship with one another, they can see and value their relationship with God. They do not hide, as we may want to do when our emotional state is low, and when they are doing well, they show up to support one another. As any strong relationship would show, members will show up even when they have nothing new to talk about, and they will support each other in their life's calling.

> *A true small group is a group of people in relationship with one another, supporting one another to remain in relationship with God together.*

A true small group consists of people who not only have regularly scheduled meetings, but they continue to speak with one another on the phone or meet for lunch outside formal gatherings. This means one-on-one availability, even during modern-day busy work hours. It is a collective friendship like you might have had as a child when you had less on your plate. Availability is required for a disciple of Jesus.

> *As any strong relationship would show, members will show up even when they have nothing new to talk about, and they will support each other in their life's calling.*

Note that our ability to be available to others also shows how available we are to God. When we are rushed throughout the day to get tasks done and have not stopped to be in relationship with others, we probably did not stop to ask God for guidance in the midst of our most important decisions.

A small group is where we learn to be disciples of Jesus so that we can make disciples of others. We cannot make new disciples when we do not know how to be disciples of Jesus ourselves. A small group is how Jesus made disciples, and small groups are how the Early Church made disciples.

We must recognize that the church has shifted in methods of operations since the Roman nationalization of the "religion" in the third century. The changes continued to follow cultural trends, including that of today's capitalistic thinking. Many churches are now run as a once-a-week activity in the minds of the public, and sometimes even in the minds of the clergy who see their roles as a job. Even some so-called Christians see a church service or event as a scheduling activity that they would attend if there are no conflicting events. To them, being the church is not really a way of life or being the salt and light of the world (Matthew 5:13–16; also, see chapter 1 of this book for Jesus's intent regarding Matthew 28:19, which is to *live out* the life of discipleship).

> *Many churches are now run as a once-a-week activity in the minds of the public, and sometimes even in the minds of the clergy who see their roles as a job.*

An Experiment to See What an Unchurched Person Seeking God Might Experience

In 2015, I ran an experiment when I moved to a new area where I did not know many people. I looked up ten local churches and tried to attend their services, whether Wednesday services, Friday services, Lord's Day services, or Bible studies. During this experiment, I tried to infer what an unchurched person who was seeking to know if God can help them with their situation might experience if they were to seek the Christian Church to find God.[154]

The unfortunate result was that eight out of ten churches did not even know I was there. I attended a mix of Korean and non-Korean churches, and often ended up sitting alone in a pew. Often no one spoke to me or showed me love. This is how unchurched people must feel when they try to reach out to Christians to ask about the God they serve; that is, if Christians even make themselves known as followers of Jesus.

The worst experience I had in one of these churches was when a pastor actually walked me out of the church while bidding me well. (That reminded me of James 2:16.) This was a church that a neighbor actually invited me to join. I visited the church website and saw that they had a Wednesday evening Bible study at 7:00 p.m., and I decided to attend. When I entered the church, I saw what looked like an exciting event occurring in the main sanctuary, and I wondered if that was where the meeting was.

I saw a sign for the senior pastor's office nearby, and as the door was slightly open, I saw that he was inside. I knocked and introduced myself as a first-time visitor. I told him that I had come because of the information I saw on their website about a meeting that night. I was surprised by the next steps, which I only realized had happened as I was driving back home.

He mentioned that the website had not been updated for a long time and that there was no meeting. He said the regular worship services are at other times and that I should come back then. He told me this as he was walking me to my car. I asked about the lively music and activities that were taking place in the main sanctuary, and he told me that some church leaders had gone through some special training and were celebrating.

For many "churched" people, such scenarios can be pictured and dismissed as something that can easily happen. However, when considered from the perspective of an unchurched person, whom Jesus calls the lost sheep—where ninety-nine sheep can be left alone to go after the one (Matthew 18:12–14), that "one" has just been rejected. That "one" may have come with a desire to know if God exists and if He would be there for them in their life's struggles, wondering if they would meet God and come to know Him when they made it to a church. Yet Christians are often not available when such people cry out, seeking God.

> *One may have come with a desire to know if God exists and if He would be there for them in their life's struggles, wondering if they would meet God and come to know Him when they made it to a church. Yet Christians are often not available when such people cry out, seeking God.*

Additionally, the gathering times that are made available to the public are often service hours, which are generally geared toward those who are already believers to come and worship God together. However, an unchurched person coming to these one-way conversations (to sit in a pew and listen to the speaker), may not receive the relationship, love, and/or answers to the questions they may be experiencing.

> *An unchurched person coming to these one-way conversations may not receive the relationship, love, and/or answers to the questions they may be experiencing.*

Rather, small groups, where Christians already practice a depth of love and more of what relationships should be, should be promoted and announced by the church as a way to invite those who are new and are simply interested. In a small group, the interested person can simply observe over time, seeing the love of Christ and coming to know and experience God. This runs counter to modern-day evangelistic views where Christians go out to supermarkets and share the gospel message, expecting the person to believe then and there (see chapter 4 about historic evangelism for more details).

In this chapter, the goal is to show biblically that love is the highest calling for Christians. This is more than "worship" itself. It is about loving God and loving others—and living that out through our lives. We will primarily look at 2 Peter 1:5–9, 1 John 4:7–8, and 1 Corinthians 13. The first two tell that love is the highest calling for Christians, while the last passage explains how we can execute this in our lives.

2 Peter 1:5–9: Our Highest Calling Is Love

> *In view of all this, make every effort to respond to God's promises. Supplement your faith with a generous provision of moral excellence, and moral excellence with knowledge, and knowledge with self-control, and self-control with patient endurance, and patient endurance with godliness, and godliness with brotherly affection, and brotherly affection with love for everyone.*
>
> *The more you grow like this, the more productive and useful you will be in your knowledge of our Lord Jesus Christ. But those who fail to develop in this way are shortsighted or blind, forgetting that they have been cleansed from their old sins.*
>
> 2 Peter 1:5–9

What do you consider to be today's cultural idol? What do many people today idolize? To give a hint, how do many people respond when you ask, "How are you doing?" The response I hear much nowadays is, "I've been busy" or "I have a lot on my plate." There are certainly responses like, "I'm fine," but they are usually given simply to brush off the formalities and to get to the topic they want to get to, or so they can move away from each other and get back to "work." The answer is *busyness*.

It is this idol of busyness that prevents people from being available for each other, or available to God. It even kills the ability to form relationships with one another and with God. Busyness that takes priority over one another and God is what we call an idol.

> *It is this idol of busyness that prevents people from being available for each other, or available to God.*

Many so-called Christians are no different in this aspect, and we wonder how the Church is different from the world when the Church simply follows along with the changing times. We are called to be holy, as God is holy; that is, we are called to be different, as He is different (1 Peter 1:14–16; Ephesians 5:1). As Christians, our calling in the busy world is to be available—to be available to God and to others. That is how people will know that we are disciples of Jesus. They will know this because of our ability to love—because we have a relationship with God that we are able to show others (John 13:35).

Peter makes this clear in this passage. Starting with verse 5 of 2 Peter 1, we can see a list of character traits in which Christians ought to grow. When we look at this list carefully, we can see a sequential list of levels of growth that require us to grow from one character trait to another until we reach the highest character trait, which is love. In picture form, here is what it looks like:

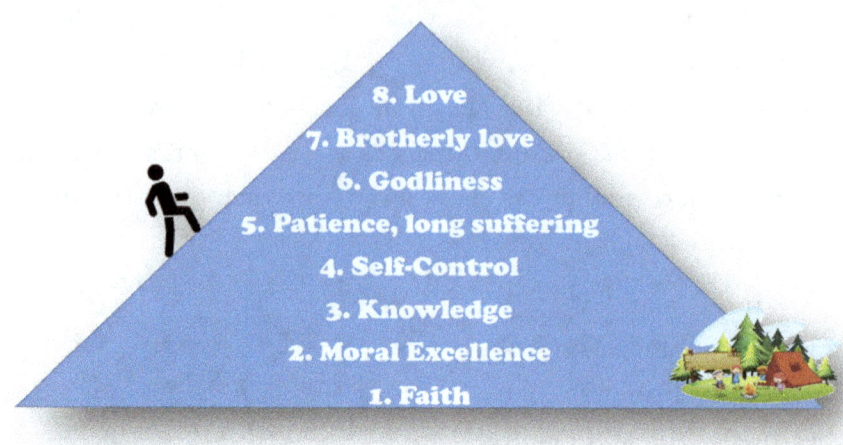

Pictorial View of Peter's Exhortations from 2 Peter 1:5–7

Understanding that these levels of growth are expected for Christians, it should be clear that many people begin at the bottom, which is the reason why the picture shows a triangle with the biggest base at the bottom. It is not easy to climb to the fullness that God desires in us (see Ephesians 4:12–16). There are less people who attain the highest goal, but it is something all Christians must try to reach.

It may take baby steps to reach maturity; however, many people tend to fall back to lower levels and stay there because it is simply easier than striving to climb. That is why there is a picture of campers having fun at the bottom of the base of the triangle. Many will settle for the lower levels, thinking they have attained what God has desired for them.

> *Many people tend to fall back to lower levels and stay there because it is simply easier than striving to climb. . . . Many will settle for the lower levels, thinking they have attained what God has desired for them.*

However, our highest calling is love. Perhaps we might try to reach the sixth level or even the seventh level in our own strength, forcing ourselves to meet with people and hope for the best as we try, but the ultimate love—agape, unconditional love—requires God's intervention to transform our hearts so that we can be able to love that way (Ezekiel 36:26–27).

Let's break down the eight levels that Peter shares with us.

Faith

Faith is certainly a necessity in our Christian walk (John 3:16; Hebrews 11:6). It is by faith that we are saved (Romans 1:17), and it is something every Christian must cling to regardless of the circumstances around them (2 Corinthians 5:7; Hebrews 11:1). However, that is only the first step in growing toward the fullness God desires for us (Ephesians 4:12–16). Faith is important, but it is also just the starting point.

It is interesting that even demons believe in God, and James tells us that having faith by itself is not sufficient. The faith must lead to fruit, or growth (James 2:19–20). Modern-day culture reduces the Christian faith by implying that anything we believe in can be done. Some even say that the "universe" wants to make our dreams come true, so we must believe.[155]

Faith, even though it is the starting point for any Christian, can be misdirected. People can accept and believe whatever they wish. They can even believe in the lies of the enemy. That is why a Christian must not settle in faith, but must aim to be more mature so as not to be *tossed and blown about by every wind of new teaching* (Ephesians 4:14).

We should also note that people tend to have faith that is fickle. They say they believe in Jesus, but then turn back as soon as their circumstances change. This is what happened between Jesus's triumphal entry and His crucifixion. The same people in that crowd who praised Jesus also shouted, "Crucify Him!" (Matthew 21:1–11; 27:22–23), sending Jesus to the cross. It is also evident that many people believe in God because of potential positive benefits they may receive, but when faced with the truth of putting one's life on the line (see Matthew 26:69–75) or denying oneself (Matthew 16:24–25) and trusting God fully for things unknown, people will desert Jesus (John 6:66).

Human faith is not as stable as we would like to believe. That is why the Bible says that even though *many began to trust in Him*, He did not trust them (John 2:23–25). That is why believers must keep growing in faith that should result in constant, unshakable faith. That kind of faith is only something God is able to provide and enable.

Moral Excellence

Many so-called Christians claim to be Christians because of the moral lives they live. They do not murder or use curse words, and they are generally nice to others. They believe that as long as they follow the moral code that they think Jesus taught, they are Christians and have eternal life.

> *Many so-called Christians claim to be Christians because of the moral lives they live.*

Many such Christians believe this, and they camp out at the second level thinking they have it under control. However, we are called Christians because of our faith in what He has done. It is not by our works or our ability to live moral lives that we are forgiven and accepted, but it is simply because of what Jesus has done; it is our trust and faith in Him that makes us Christians (e.g., John 3:16; Ephesians 2:1–10).

Romans 3:19–27 explains that the moral law simply shows us that we are incapable of executing it perfectly. It shows us that trying to attain perfection only leads to the recognition that we fall short. That is why we need a savior, Jesus Christ. Verse 25 clearly says that our moral goodness does not suffice, but that *people are made right with God when they believe that Jesus sacrificed His life, shedding His blood.*

As Christians, we ought to show moral excellence, but that is neither the basis of our being called Christians, nor is it the ultimate goal for Christians. It is simply something we do as a result of the love that we have received from God. Let us not settle for being morally good, especially as many people, even those who do not believe in God, may be able to live morally good lives. As Christians, we are called to something more.

Knowledge

Some cultures, such as the Korean culture, tend to over-elevate the importance of education. It is sometimes elevated so highly that people who come to know God may get misdirected to leave their secular professions/businesses once they become a Christian and go to seminary to study to become a pastor. Cultural elevation of education may lead well-intentioned believers the wrong way.

Fortunately, this is where the relief comes in: knowledge is only the third level. This also implies that not every "Christian" pastor is truly Christian. Nor do seminary degrees mean that a person is a disciple of Jesus Christ. It is important for believers to grow in their knowledge of Christ—to study the Word of God and solidly understand the basis of their faith; however, even gaining such knowledge is not their ultimate calling.

I have spoken with many seminary students, and I have come to realize that some of them have chosen to attend seminary because of a misunderstanding of what it means to grow in Christ. Some pastors I know say they became a pastor because things were not working out well in their previous jobs, and they felt that being a pastor was a good career choice. Sadly, many pastors today have not been called to their roles, but have become pastors due to a misunderstanding, thinking that being a pastor will bring them closer to God. Many Christians may also wrongly think that their roles in the marketplace, whether as businessmen, engineers, doctors, or architects, are not God-ordained callings, when in fact such abilities enable them to reach the world (for more details, see chapter 5 on the use of business models to reach the less accessible).

The Bible is clear that knowledge in itself only leads to pride, but love should be the goal (1 Corinthians 8:1). Paul also talks about how knowledge does not compare to truly knowing Christ as Lord (Philippians 3:3–14).

Knowledge is important, but it is not the highest goal for a Christian. People with graduate degrees or professional certifications should not boast of their accomplishments, but should rather use their learning, abilities, and experience to support the Church in love. This also implies that the teaching from pastors must go beyond head knowledge, but should also inspire others to truly love God and neighbors more.

> *People with graduate degrees or professional certifications should not boast of their accomplishments, but should rather use their learning, abilities, and experience to support the Church in love.*

Knowledge of God and His Word, is very important, and growing in this knowledge should be a daily practice (Psalm 1:2).

However, when Christians feel that they know the Scriptures or perhaps feel good because they have the discipline to read several chapters daily, they may simply be puffed up with pride (Luke 18:9–14). Knowledge in itself is not the highest calling for Christians, and there is more than just daily readings and knowledge accumulated over time. Let us not be like many educated people who claim to be Christians because of their knowledge as they settle here.

Self-Control

Self-control, or discipline, is a good thing, but it is still not our highest calling. Those who settle at this level are people who attend every Lord's Day, Wednesday, and Friday church service, and perhaps even morning services for the Korean crowd. They are able to discipline themselves to read the Bible daily and keep themselves from sins that may be visible to others. Remember that Peter tells us that all eight levels are good and necessary for Christians, but the call here is to not settle until we reach the highest level that God desires us to attain.

The apostle Paul tells us in 1 Corinthians 9:19–27 that there is a clear purpose to doing what one does (see verse 26). In the latter verses (vv. 23–27), Paul says that he disciplines himself like an athlete to bring people to Christ. If the purpose of the self-control is solely to boast in one's ability to maintain oneself, then that would simply be pride like that of the proud Pharisee (Luke 18:9–14). Paul's purpose in self-discipline was to love others by sharing the Good News, which is the love of Christ.

Self-control is certainly a character trait in a mature Christian. The apostle Paul writes to Titus about what it means to be an elder—someone who oversees other Christians in living the right way. He emphasizes that it is right for an elder, or any Christian maturing in faith, to be self-disciplined and grow in knowledge (Titus 1:6–9). It is important as a follower of Jesus to be disciplined in order to avoid sinful behaviors of the world and to represent Christ correctly. It will be this self-discipline that will keep a Christian in prayer when busyness comes about (1 Peter 4:7). It will be this self-discipline that will enable the person to sing hymns even when caught in a bind (Acts 16:25). Christians need self-discipline.

However, just being disciplined does not mean that you are a Christian. A Christian must continue to grow beyond just faith, morality, knowledge, and self-control. This is only the fourth level of the progressive Christian growth.

Patience

The word "patience" here is ὑπομονήν (hupomonen). It refers to enduring over time—or more literally, remaining under and bearing the weight for some time. In the culture of maximizing efficiency and minimizing time to produce the same results, relationships take a heavy beating.

In the culture of maximizing efficiency and minimizing time to produce the same results, relationships take a heavy beating.

Every meeting, including church services or even small groups, apparently needs a clear time to begin and end for most participants. If the meeting happens to go longer than the expected time, people will either leave in order to make their next appointments or will complain that the activity went over the allotted time.

However, relationships cannot be constrained by time limitations. Relationships take time. They are not something to be rushed. Small-group meetings should have a definite start time and a rough estimated end time, but it should not be time blocked.[156] Additionally, the small groups should have a recurring time to meet so that members know to schedule around that time, knowing also to leave the end time open so they can enjoy unhurried time together.

Note also that perseverance is a character of love (1 Corinthians 13:4, 7). It refers to being patient, or bearing with one another over time. Love cannot occur in an instant. Evangelism, or being a witness to another person about Christ, can only be done in the context of love, which takes time.

> *Evangelism, or being a witness to another person about Christ, can only be done in the context of love, which takes time.*

This is why street evangelism is less effective. Certainly, we dare not limit God in what He can do through short encounters, but our call to make disciples is to love others over time. The right way to execute evangelism is to invite and welcome people who may be interested in God so that they can observe the lives of Christians over time without any pressure. As they see people over and over again who may be similar to them and who go to God for all their needs, able to continue their lives with great joy, the interested person, too, may come to believe. The key factor is that love must be shared over time, and it may take a while. That is why love is patient.

However, patience in itself is not the Christian's highest calling. There are still more levels to climb.

Godliness

Godliness refers to living a holy life. The opposite of godliness would be godless living or living as if God does not exist (Titus 2:12). Holiness refers to living differently (set apart) from the rest of the world. As God is holy, we too are to be holy in the way we live (1 Peter 1:15–16). In other words, just as God is different, so we are called to be different from the rest of the world.[157]

To reiterate, the eight items on this list are all good and necessary for Christians; however, we should not settle at a lower level, believing that the lower level is our ultimate calling. Many people may settle with having faith; others might even live moral lives and consider that sufficient. However, as Christians, we must continue to grow to the *full and complete* measure of Christ (Ephesians 4:12–16), which leads us back to Him, who is love (1 John 4:7–8).

In a negative sense, some may think of godliness as an outward activity such as attending church services. Some people might think of godliness as becoming a pastor and preaching from the pulpit frequently.

> *If these activities take precedence over the higher calling of love, they would be meaningless*

God might use some of us in this way, but this is still not our highest calling. If these activities take precedence over the higher calling of love, they would be meaningless (1 Corinthians 13:1–3).

As an example of godliness gone wrong, consider Luke 18:9–14, as well as those who attend seminary even though they have not been called by God. Also consider 1 Timothy 6:5–6, where Paul talks about *a show of godliness* in contrast to *true godliness*.

Of course, the right view of godliness is to desire to please God in all that we do, including in our worship, in our workplaces, in how we treat our neighbors, and in how united we are with the family God has given us. It is

> *Godliness is to desire to please God in all that we do . . . and to have the heart of worship that desires to seek God in community with brothers and sisters who love Jesus.*

more than faithfully attending church services, but it is *to have the heart of worship* that desires to seek God in community with brothers and sisters who love Jesus. Paul even tells us that training in godliness has eternal benefits (1 Timothy 4:7–8).

To be clear, even though worship is important, that *act of worship* is not the highest calling. In many Asian churches (and also in some other cultures), attendance to worship services is considered to be of great importance. When such churches say they have small groups, they gather a few people together to follow a prescribed method of worship that is no different than their regular worship service. The focus in these small groups is not on love, relationships, or discipleship, but rather is on the replication of worship that is held on the Lord's Day during a church service. These small groups can easily be identified by observing who shares the message. In such small groups, it is often the pastor who must be present in order for the small group to proceed. It is not a mutual sharing of lives, but is simply meeting for yet another unilateral message. However, love takes precedence over acts of worship.

> *Love takes precedence over acts of worship.*

Worship is important, and it should be in the front of our minds in all that we do. However, when that is identified as acts of godliness such as praying before every meal, reading the Scriptures daily, and faithful attendance to church services—they are certainly good—but it is not the highest calling for followers of Jesus.

Consider what Samuel says to Saul in 1 Samuel 15:22: "But Samuel replied, 'What is more pleasing to the Lord: your burnt offerings and sacrifices or your obedience to his voice? Listen! Obedience is better than sacrifice, and submission is better than offering the fat of rams.'" Saul figured that doing prescribed

> *True worship is a matter of the heart where believers express their true love for God.*

worship services for God was the *proper task* to keep God happy, but that was certainly not the case. Acts of godliness may not lead to true worship, where true worship is a matter of the heart (Romans 12:1–2) where believers express their *true love* for God.

Godliness is important, but we must remember that it is not the highest calling. Being faithful in attending worship services without the next step is like being a noisy gong or a clanging cymbal (1 Corinthians 13:1–2). Our greatest calling, our greatest commandment, is to love (Matthew 22:36–40).

Love, Brotherly Love

There are two kinds of love mentioned in this passage: *philia* and *agape*. The actual word used here is Φιλαδελφία (*Philadelphia*), or the "love of brothers." Yes, that is what the famous city in Pennsylvania is named after. Brotherly love may project different concepts for different people. To set the right frame, perhaps it is good to point to childhood, when siblings are living under the care of parents and cannot go separate ways of their own accord. There is a certain bond in living together that goes beyond childhood, even after they separate from their parents and move on to start their own families.

However, this biblical commitment to grow directs Christians to do so with people beyond one's family. How can this love be formed? It has to do with returning to what has been learned in childhood, and that is the concept of brotherhood (or sisterhood), or even the term *friendship*, which has lost its original meaning due to instant "likes" in social media today (consider Matthew 24:12, which says that *the love of many will grow cold*). Generation Y or older generations may remember a time when, as children, they spent much time with the same friends and shared much of their lives together with one another. Such concepts do not seem to exist for younger generations today.

In modern days, busyness, or having things to do, seems to hold a greater priority. The call for Christians is to live life together—perhaps not living in the same house, but living life together through continually gathering together (Hebrews 10:25) and knowing one another deeply as a result.

Brotherhood (or sisterhood) has the opposite connotation from that of social media living. In social media, people often project only positive images or thoughts about themselves. "Friends" in social media are often considered to be people who are connected either by brief encounters or by being connected by second or third degrees. However, true friendship, or brotherhood, goes beyond surface-level knowledge of one another. True friends know what the other person is going through, where their life's pursuits lie, and where they struggle the most. Friendships cannot occur without intentional life-on-life interactions, which means that intentional recurring meetings take place, even when there are no new reasons, but simply to connect. This is the call for Christians.

> *True friends know what the other person is going through, where their life's pursuits lie, and where they struggle the most.*

Growing Christians are to be relationship-focused and should even go out of their way to meet one another and spend time with them. They would do this regardless of whether there is a purpose to the meeting, and that—the relationships—is the crux of small groups.

The call is for Christians to love one another (1 Peter 1:22), and this love will be seen by

> *Love must take greater priority.*

people outside the Church (John 13:35). The problem, of course, is that many Christians do not aim for this level of growth, but remain in the lower levels, thinking they have attained what it means to be a Christian. That is why many "churches" today are without love, but are more focused on religious aspects. Love must take greater priority.

Operating genuine small groups is not easy—because love is not easy for humans, which is also the reason why many Christians shy away from it. When Satan grabs a foothold, a Christian may

> *Love and busyness do not go together.*

think, "I have a lot on my plate today" or "I am not feeling as confident today, and I do not want to let my guard down." There can be many reasons why Christians may be tempted to skip the patience component of love, and this goes back to the cultural idol, which is busyness.[158] Love and busyness do not go together.

It is for that reason that small groups must meet frequently, with or without a reason, to continue to develop and build relationships with one

> *As Christians make themselves available for others, they are making themselves available for God to direct, guide, and use.*

another. It is also important to recognize that as people become independent, or lack relationships with others, they will also have that same lack of relationship with Jesus. The opposite holds true too; as Christians make themselves available for others, they are making themselves available for God to direct, guide, and use (Matthew 25:36–40).

God gave us one another so that we can know what it means to be in a relationship with Him. Consider a husband and wife compared to Jesus and the Church (Ephesians 5:21–33), or consider that what we do for others, we are doing for God (Matthew 25:37–40). Christians must continue to gather together in small groups frequently to develop the *philia* love.

> *God gave us one another so that we can know what it means to be in a relationship with Him.*

We might think that *philia* love is difficult to attain, but there is a higher calling still, which is the hardest for limited human beings to understand or attain.

Love—Agape Love

This is a Christian's highest calling—unconditional love. This is not just any kind of love, but it is the love that comes only from God (1 John 4:7–21). Ἀγάπην (*agape*) love is what all Christians must aspire to. This level of love does not come by works, but is given only by God through His grace.

The other seven steps might be accomplished through practice and discipline such as attending small groups weekly, striving hard to maintain a heart of worship, bearing with people who take up your time, and so forth. However, the highest calling of love is not something we can attain on our own.

Agape love is the ability to love God with all our heart, soul, mind, and strength, and also to love others—even our enemies (Matthew 5:43–47; 22:37–40). As humans, we are limited in our ability to love that far or that deeply, but it is through God's grace that we are able to love our enemies or even those we do not know. Even in the midst of the busy world that may be filled with chaos, we can love God with all our heart, soul, mind, and strength.

> *Agape love is the ability to love God with all our heart, soul, mind, and strength, and also to love others—even our enemies.*

This is the covenantal promise of Ezekiel 36:26–27, where God says He will transform our hardened hearts to enable us to keep His regulations by enabling us to love God and others so that we can keep the Greatest Commandment.

Christians aspiring to this level of growth must have their faith in Jesus to come and help them. Agape love can only come through full dependence on God, especially as Christians continue to live out the other seven levels of Christian living. Only God is able to enable us to love Him with all our hearts and to love others as ourselves.

The State of the Church Today

Based on Peter's teachings, it is clear that love is our highest calling. However, love is not what the Church is known for. This is because many Christians have settled at a lower level than the highest calling. This shows in the way many Christians live and even in their teachings.

Before Abraham was called to go to the promised land of Canaan (Genesis 12:1), his father actually had the calling. However, his father, Terah, failed to get there. He started the journey

> *He started the journey and began moving in that direction, but he stopped short. He settled. . . . He failed to fulfill his calling.*

and began moving in that direction, but he stopped short. He settled. Genesis 11:31–32 shares this sad news:

> *One day Terah took his son Abram, his daughter-in-law Sarai (his son Abram's wife), and his grandson Lot (his son Haran's child) and moved away from Ur of the Chaldeans. He was headed for the land of Canaan, but they stopped at Haran and settled there. Terah lived for 205 years and died while still in Haran.*

We see that Terah headed toward Canaan with Abram, Sarai, and Lot. Instead of continuing the journey, though, he *settled* in Haran and died there. Terah missed the call. He failed to fulfill his calling. As a result, God had to reassign this special call to another person, Terah's son.

It is the same with many Christians. God has a calling for them, but they settle for something less than what God calls them to. They settle at different levels and believe they have fulfilled their life's calling. Some settle for having faith, some for living a good life, some for having great knowledge with degrees and certifications, and some for being highly disciplined.

Local church leaders, too, may settle. They may teach about being patient and perhaps place much focus on living a holy life and attending worship services. Sadly, many Christians do not go after the love that God has called us to.

Have you settled? Has your church settled? Is your highest pursuit love?

Rationally, there is some logic to why people settle. Love, especially agape love, is difficult to attain. For one thing, we cannot bring it about ourselves, as this is something only God is able to provide for us. Even the levels below that are not very easy to live out and maintain. Brotherly love is not easy, and maintaining godliness is difficult. How long can we go before we commit another sin to nullify our godliness? Patience is hard too. So are all the others.

That is why people camp out at the lower levels, at a level they feel they can justify, such as faith or moral excellence. Since they are able to justify their positions to themselves, they believe they are good enough and that God should consider them good enough for being so. However, just as Abraham was an imperfect person who had to learn over time through experience, God disciplines those whom He loves (Proverbs 3:12; Hebrews 12:6). God desires His followers to grow to the fullest and to pursue their highest calling, which is love.

> *That is why people camp out at the lower levels, at a level they feel they can justify.*

1 John 4:7–8: God Is Love

> *Dear friends, let us continue to love one another, for love comes from God. Anyone who loves is a child of God and knows God. But anyone who does not love does not know God, for God is love.*
>
> 1 John 4:7–8

The One who calls us His children is Love Himself. We are called children of God because of His love in us. Our highest calling is love, and those who do not love do not know God.

This may be a direct correlation to Matthew 7:21–23. In this passage, Jesus will say, *I never knew you* to those who did not do the will of the Father. The will of the Father is written all throughout the Scriptures and is summarized in the Greatest Commandment, which is derived from the Ten Commandments, and is also implied in the

Great Commission. The will of the Father is to love Him foremost and to love others. Jesus even adds that those who love Him do what He commands (John 14:23–24). His command to love is shared in the next chapter of John, where Jesus says, *This is my commandment: Love each other in the same way I have loved you* (John 15:12; see also verses 13, 14, and 17).

John 13:35 says that people will know the true followers of Jesus by their love. If evangelism is on one's heart, love must be one's highest pursuit.

Sadly, many Christians and local church leaders do not place love as their highest goal, and that is why people no longer associate love with Christians. When people find themselves lost, hurt, or seeking love and acceptance, they turn somewhere else other than to the Church.

> *When people find themselves lost, hurt, or seeking love and acceptance, they turn somewhere else other than to the Church.*

First John 4:7–8 teaches us that we ought to love one another. This refers to love among Christians. This is critical in demonstrating God's love to people who do not believe in Jesus. It is by love among one another that we are able to extend that love to the outside world. Love is all connected, for love is God Himself. To truly love God, other Christians, or not-yet-Christians, that love must be initiated by and accomplished by God, who is love.

John clearly states that we cannot love God while we hate our brother (or sister) (1 John 4:20). That is why Jesus even adds that we should reconcile relationships with others before coming to God (Matthew 5:23–24). We cannot love God without being able to love others. If we cannot love other Christian brothers and sisters—sharing lives over time—how can we possibly love those who do not believe in Jesus? In other words, how can we say we love God and share our lives with Him if we do not love others and share our lives with them (Matthew 25:37–40)?

God has given us one another so that we can learn and experience what it is to be in relationship with the invisible God. Our ability to love others reflects our ability to love God. Our ability to share lives together with others over time shows the depth of relationship we can have with God.

> *Our ability to love others reflects our ability to love God. Our ability to share lives together with others over time shows the depth of relationship we can have with God.*

Now how can we describe love? This is shown in the chapter that is known as the Love Chapter—1 Corinthians 13.

1 Corinthians 13: Love in Practice

> *If I could speak all the languages of earth and of angels, but didn't love others, I would only be a noisy gong or a clanging cymbal. If I had the gift of prophecy, and if I understood all of God's secret plans and possessed all knowledge, and if I had such faith that I could move mountains, but didn't love others, I would be nothing. If I gave everything I have to the poor and even sacrificed my body, I could boast about it; but if I didn't love others, I would have gained nothing.*
>
> *Love is patient and kind. Love is not jealous or boastful or proud or rude. It does not demand its own way. It is not irritable, and it keeps no record of being wronged. It does not rejoice about injustice but rejoices whenever the truth wins out. Love never gives up, never loses faith, is always hopeful, and endures through every circumstance. Prophecy and speaking in*

unknown languages and special knowledge will become useless. But love will last forever! . . . Three things will last forever—faith, hope, and love—and the greatest of these is love.

1 Corinthians 13:1–8, 13

The apostle Paul was a highly educated and renowned person who held important decision-making roles in the synagogues (see Acts 8:3; 22:3). A person like Paul could possibly be compared to a chief executive of a modern-day corporation. A person with this kind of stature might be expected to be driving the bottom line or efficiency of a business or system process. Nonetheless, Paul states that everything is meaningless if love is not the foremost and highest pursuit.

The first three verses in 1 Corinthians 13 refer to three things that Christians highly value. The first is knowledge. Someone can be very educated and speak many languages, which is certainly important in the work of making disciples of all nations, yet Paul says this is only a *noisy gong or a clanging cymbal* if love is excluded.

The second thing refers to gifting. Through spiritual gifts, people can hear from God and experience His love. Yet even with the benefits of spiritual gifting, especially toward one another, Paul says it is *nothing* if it is not accompanied by love.

The third refers to service. Giving to others and helping others in need in practice is very necessary in demonstrating the love of Christ. Yet even with faith in works (James 2:17–18), Paul says it gains him nothing without love.

> *What is the differentiator between whether or not it is pleasing and acceptable to God? The one thing that must exist is love.*

What is the differentiator between whether or not it is pleasing and acceptable to God? The one thing that must exist is love.

This shows that Christians, no matter how well-intended, can do all things without love. This includes students studying for the Lord and businesspeople running their businesses for the Lord. It also includes Christians who lead revival meetings and conferences, and those who receive prayer from spiritual leaders for the sake of focusing on improving their spiritual gifting. It also includes people serving in mission organizations, along with other acts of goodwill. All of these people might believe that God would be pleased with their activities, but it is possible that God does not give them credit for their actions if they are operating without love. Their works are not accepted by God if they do not have love.

> *All of these people might believe that God would be pleased with their activities, but it is possible that God does not give them credit for their actions if they are operating without love.*

A Christian must grow in relationship with God, and that growth shows that the person is indeed a child of God (Deuteronomy 8:5; Hebrews 12:7–10; Revelation 3:19). Growth in love toward one another, both toward believers and not-yet-believers, demonstrates that our love for the Lord is growing (Matthew 25:37–40).

So then, let us get down to the practical: what is love? First Corinthians 13:4–7 tells us what love is, and this is a description of *agape* love. Love may seem nice, but as 1 Corinthians 13 explains, it is the most difficult thing to do in practice. In fact, I would propose that it is impossible to do perfectly. We need the grace of God to cover our mistakes while He enables us to love.

As we go through this passage, consider how these characteristics of love would show up for a small group of people who meet frequently and share lives together. The first item on the list is, of course, one of the most difficult aspects, especially in today's time-constrained environment.

Love is patient. (v. 4)

The word *patient* is the Greek word μακροθυμέω (*makrothmeo*), which means "suffering for a long time." The King James Version actually uses the words "suffers long" instead of the more common and positive-sounding word "patient."

In our modern society, patience is a misnomer in many cases. Christians sometimes say a prayer request for patience, but their mindset and the world they live in is full of busyness or is in pursuit of efficiency. Patience is not easy to find, nor is it praised in the real world. The business-minded world looks for impacts and results, not something like patience that seems to produce nothing tangible.

This word *patient* means to bear with one another over a long time. Love is not a one-time visit to the prison or food shelter, nor is it going on a short-term missions trip for a week to run a Bible program. If a relationship ends after a short time, then it is a project, not love.[159]

> *If a relationship ends after a short time, then it is a project, not love.*

Patience also has the connotation of being slow to anger, to bear with the difficulties of the person, and to hold faith in the person despite the slow progress or lack of it. It is life-sharing that includes the good times and the bad, the successes and the failures—a definition of friendship that has lost meaning during the past decades. Today, it is easier to see people wanting to make a maximum impact for strangers and feel good about themselves after having tried. That is not love, but perhaps is something riddled with pride.

Love is kind. (v. 4)

Kindness. The word used for *kindness* is χρηστεύομαι (*chresteuomai*). It means to be good and to be of useful service to others.[160] *Kindness*, like *patience*, is a word that can be easy to say and

> *Kindness is very difficult in practice because it means to do good toward others when they are not worthy of it.*

can be easy to believe that one has such a characteristic, but in truth, kindness is very difficult in practice because it means to do good to others when they are not worthy of it. It requires us to be merciful and to take a beating when we do not deserve it for the benefit of another.

Consider Genesis 50:14–21. Joseph's brothers knew they had wronged their younger brother, and Joseph was now the man in charge—not just of their lives, but of their children as well. Their father had just passed away, and they were rightfully afraid of the punishment they might receive from the person they had wronged. They even tried a clever ploy to tell Joseph that his father said to forgive his brothers (Genesis 50:16–17). Then they bowed before him, seeking mercy (Genesis 50:18). Joseph showed kindness by forgiving his brothers and assuring them that they and their children would be taken care of (Genesis 50:21). This kindness was certainly not necessary, for the brothers deserved wrath from the one they tried to kill.

This same story repeats itself in many places in the Bible, such as when Saul thanked David for his kindness for not killing him when he had the chance (1 Samuel 24:18–19). This was the same even with Jesus toward us sinners. It is not because we deserved God's forgiveness that we are forgiven, but it is because of His grace (Romans 3:24: 11:5–6; Ephesians 2:1–10). That is the kindness of God, and Jesus calls us to show that same kindness to others (Luke 10:37; Ephesians 4:32).

Kindness also refers to treating others differently than we normally would, or differently than the world's standards. Consider Joshua 6:23–25: Rahab and her family got special kind treatment from Israel when her nation was to be completely destroyed. There may be special people whom God instructs us to treat differently, even though they may be undeserving of it. This same kindness is found in Ruth, who, as a stranger living in poverty, was given permission to pick grain from a land that was not hers (Ruth 2). The opposite of kindness would be cruelty or oppression toward those in weaker positions (Proverbs 11:17).

We certainly cannot miss the story about Mephibosheth, Saul's grandson who was lame (2 Samuel 9). Mephibosheth was not able to serve David due to being lame, nor did he have a good history, having a grandfather who chased David, trying to kill him. Yet kindness is given to someone who cannot give anything back. This goes along with Jesus telling us to do the same (Luke 14:12–14).

Consider a modern example. You welcome a family that does not have a lot of money into your home. You receive very little from them as you give them access to your entire

> *Kindness says to take the beating and trust God for more blessings.*

home, including your spacious private quarters. Yet you see them have the windows open on a nice cool day while also having the air conditioner on. Kindness says to take the beating and trust God for more blessings. Thinking with a business mindset, following the trend of today's times, one would perhaps react with anger and threats and might even ask them to leave.

I use this example because this is the kind of situation that affluent Christian leaders might face today. Would you be kind to others as Jesus was to you? Perhaps the key lesson for those to whom God has given resources would be to let go and let God provide. Be kind and merciful to those who do not deserve it, and trust God to bring about justice when those to whom you are kind return abuse to you.

Kindness goes beyond the people we know and those who are good to us. That is the message of Jesus in Matthew 5:47. Paul says the same to Timothy when he says that a servant of the Lord must be kind to *everyone* (2 Timothy 2:24). How can we give the special treatment of kindness to everyone? We certainly cannot do this on our own, but God can enable us to do so. That is why agape love is not something we can do of our own accord.

Additionally, kindness is a special lesson that must be learned by all disciples of Jesus who are called to kingly roles, because kindness is often given from someone of higher authority, and God uses the kingly characteristics of His followers to administer His kindness.[161]

Love is not jealous, boastful, or proud. (v. 4)

These traits could be taken separately, but they seem to make most sense when placed together. They are basic to human nature. They are sinful characteristics of people that are difficult to avoid. All three of these are about a "me" perspective. Jealousy says that you have something or some ability that I do not have, and therefore I hate you. Pride says that I have something or some ability *you* do not have. Boasting is simply sharing about one's pride. In a sense, it is all about one's concept of desiring to become God, whether it is due to a lack of something, which leads to jealousy, or thinking that they are better than others, which leads to pride and boasting.

ζηλόω (zeloó) is the word for *jealousy* in this verse. This word actually means to burn with zeal for something. This can be used in a positive sense, but in this verse, because there is an οὐ (*ou*), which means *not* ("love is *not* . . ."), it says that love is *not* where one puts greater or greatest zeal for something else other than the original target of love.

This may remind you of the first four of the Ten Commandments: (1) God is God, (2) you shall have no other gods, (3) you shall not make anything in place of God, and (4) you shall not make God's name be used in vain. All four of these are broken, in addition to the tenth commandment, by jealousy, because this comes from a person's desire to be God. It comes from one's desire to be perfect and to be without any need.

When we see another person having more than we have, the desire for that thing or those abilities takes over. The result of jealousy is a broken relationship with the person who has that ability or thing, along with a desire for more things on earth, or separation from God.

Jealousy is part of our human nature, for all people have a natural desire to not deny themselves, but to receive the glory and honor that is due to God. All people, both poor and affluent, of different races or cultures, and even of any age, can be jealous.

Consider who might be more susceptible to being jealous. People hungry for power, whether they have little or much, can be jealous because they have not achieved absolute power, for they always want more. A jealous person who has much might belittle those who do not have much as they hoard more for themselves, while a person who loves will show kindness by caring for and giving to those who might not be deserving.

Jealousy also exists in people who rebel, whether they rebel against God, government, or authorities above them, whether at work or at church. For the most part, people rebel because they feel *they are God* and should be treated in a way that they believe they deserve. An alternative would be to accept others who are trying to lead, along with a willingness to comply. Similar to how love toward one another affects love for God, those who have difficulty working with people above them may have authority issues with God. Jealousy is anger or frustration because of what one does not have, or it can be a lack of trust in God for His sufficient provision as we try to carry out God's great calling.

> *Jealousy is anger or frustration because of what one does not have, or it can be a lack of trust in God for His sufficient provision as we try to carry out God's great calling.*

Examples of jealousy are abundant throughout the Scriptures, including Cain killing his brother (Genesis 4:8), Sarah asking her husband to dismiss her servant Hagar, even though Hagar did not have much to live on (Genesis 16:5–6), and King Saul going after David because many people seemed to praise him (1 Samuel 18:7–8).

Love does not envy. This means that our hearts are always grateful, even when someone has something more than we have. We praise God together when someone succeeds in something, and we do so over and over again. We are grateful for the talents and abilities God has given us. We are also grateful for all the resources He has given us. We believe that God can use either of us, or others beyond us, to fulfill His purposes.

Περπερεύομαι (*perpereuomai*) means to boast, and φυσιόω (*phusióo*) means "arrogant or puffed up." They both have the οὐ (*ou*) in front of them, signifying that these are not characteristics of love. It probably seems obvious, though, that those characteristics are against God and would not align with love since God is love (1 John 4:7–8).

Boasting and arrogance go along with jealousy in that they are rooted in the desire to become God. In arrogance, or pride, there is both high pride and low pride. Pastor Min Chung defines high pride as having a high view of yourself, or perhaps to consider yourself to be God because of all the success you have had. Low pride refers to a low view of yourself, as if to want to be pitied and to desire to be lifted up by others.[162] Both types of pride fall into this category, and the heart of pride can belong to those who have much or little, are young or old, or are of any culture. This heart has even existed in angels, as Lucifer rebelled against God in his pride (Isaiah 14:12–14).

There are many stories of pride in the Bible, including the story of Israel, which involved many cycles of pride against God when things were good, and turning back to God when their land was being taken by their enemies (see the book of Judges for concise examples of those cycles). Jesus taught that those who have pride are not justified, while those who come to God in humility are justified (Luke 18:14).

In short, love is hard because we all have a tendency to want to be in power, to be in control, and to be praised by others. These things belong to God, though, and not to us. We have a natural desire to

> *Love is hard because we all have a tendency to want to be in power, to be in control, and to be praised by others. These things belong to God and not to us.*

Our Highest Calling is Love

want to take that glory away from God, and continuing in these things can only turn us away from God, the source of love. The same occurs with our behavior toward others. Our desire to become God turns us away from serving them, for we tend to focus on ourselves. As a result, our relationship with one another is damaged.

Agape love is impossible to attain on our own. We need God's grace and mercy to cleanse us, and we need the empowerment of the Holy Spirit to carry us beyond our human ability so that we can truly love.

> *We need God's grace and mercy to cleanse us, and we need the empowerment of the Holy Spirit to carry us beyond our human ability so that we can truly love.*

Love is not rude and does not demand its own way. (v. 5)

Οὐκ ἀσχημονεῖ (*ouk aschmonei*) is often translated as "not rude." It refers to acting in an immoral manner or becoming that way, or showing disgrace. In the Old Testament, the idea refers to when a person is naked and disgraced (Ezekiel 16:7, 22, 39). In the same sense, a person whipped with more than forty lashes can be humiliated and disgraced (Deuteronomy 25:3). In 1 Corinthians 7:36, the "disgraceful manner" refers to desiring a woman in a sexual way.

In a practical sense, loving by not being rude is not for our own personal comfort, but for decency in relationships. For example, a person may want to

> *Love nourishes interactions and deepens relationships.*

walk around half-naked, but if it is less comfortable for others and prevents comfort in a relationship, it is not love. Rather, love nourishes interactions and deepens relationships. This can also be the case for having gender-based small groups to allow for depth in relationships without fear of inappropriate or undesired attraction.

Οὐ ζητεῖ τὰ ἑαυτῆς (*ou zetei ta hautes*) means to "not seek self," or a love that does not seek one's own way. First Corinthians 13:5 refers to love not demanding its own way. It is connected to rudeness in that not seeking or demanding one's own way is not for the purpose of personal gain, but for the sake of others.

Those who seek for their own pleasure are, as mentioned above regarding pride, seeking to be God. That is why the apostle John says to not love the world or things in it, because God is not in those people who seek personal glory (1 John 2:15–17). Those who follow Jesus deny themselves and follow in His footsteps of loving God and others (Matthew 16:24).

Love is not irritable, and it keeps no record of being wronged. (v. 5)

In the New Living Translation and some other Bible versions, this verse might be incorrectly perceived to mean that love should not irritate others. Rather, it means that when there is love, the one who gives love does not get irritated or provoked by whatever response follows from the recipient of love. The Greek words are οὐ παροξύνεται (*oun paroxunetai*), which means "not provoked."

Love is not irritable or easily provoked. It means to not be offended. That which offends God all throughout Scripture is sin, or rebellion against Him (see Numbers 15:30; 20:24; Psalm 106:29, etc.). However, God's love for His people never fails. Additionally, this same provoking, or feeling of offense, is what the Holy Spirit stirs up in us when God is offended by the sin around us (Acts 17:16).

Just as God hates sin, we, too, must hate sin. However, just as God looks beyond the sin and loves the person, so we must look beyond the sin and love the person who is loved by God. Additionally, just as God loves us and desires us to come to Him in humility and repentance, we ought to let our brothers and sisters in Christ know about any sin in their lives that they may not see, and we should do so out of love. Their response is between them and God, and we should not be offended by whatever they return back to us. At the same time, our love for them, including being there for them over time (in patience), does not cease. We should expect, too, that if they love God and us, they will tell us about any sin in our lives that we might not see, and we should not react in offense, but should be receptive to their words, recognizing their loving-kindness.

Love does not account for wrongs. Οὐ λογίζεται τὸ κακόν (*ou logizetai toe kakon*) actually means that love does not think (calculate) evil of the other person. The first word (*logizetai*) has the same root as the word *logic*, which means to calculate out or to think through the data and identify patterns. So then, even though it certainly includes the meaning of not accounting for past wrongs, it also means to not consider anyone in a bad way because of their past patterns, data, or history, or perhaps even his or her present state of mind or actions.

This is not easy at many levels, and we need God to enable us to do this. Consider a person who has spent much of their past in prostitution or pornography. Loving that person just as they are may not be easy. Additionally, those who have grown up in dire situations of abuse, such as being trafficked as a child or living on the streets without parents, may not have much trust in even the kindest Christians. Trying to bring them to a place of acceptance and trust in others, which is how they can learn to trust in God, would not be easy.[163] It will require help from God for Christians to love them patiently and without thinking bad of them, especially if they react to the givers in abuse or rebellion. Perhaps a good example would be parents who adopt and are able to love their adopted children as their very own.

We know that God did the same for us. He first provided a temporary way to be in relationship with Him, which was by animal sacrifices, in which the sacrifices atoned for sins. These laws were imperfect and did not permanently mend the relationship with God. As a result, He came to earth Himself and died, providing a permanent sacrifice so that we could be in relationship with God forever—the meaning of *Immanuel*. God no longer holds our sinfulness and our negative past against us (Hebrews 8:12–13).

Love does not rejoice about injustice, but rejoices whenever the truth wins out. (v. 6)

Οὐ χαίρει ἐπὶ τῇ ἀδικίᾳ, συγχαίρει δὲ τῇ ἀληθείᾳ (*ou chirei epi te adikia sugchairei de te alatheia*) says that love does not rejoice (οὐ χαίρει) with/over the unrighteous (ἀδικίᾳ), but rejoices (συγχαίρει) with the truth (ἀληθείᾳ).

The word *rejoice* is the same word used in Jesus's parable of the shepherd who found his one lost sheep (Matthew 18:13). It is a great rejoicing that might be accompanied by celebrations and feasting with many people. John the Baptist also equates it with a wedding ceremony where the best man would rejoice in the success of the groom (John 3:29).

The word *unrighteousness* in the Scriptures often refers to sin or injustice (e.g., Romans 9:14; 1 John 5:17). The word *truth* is used in many places in Scripture to denote the absolute truth. The *truth* tends to refer to the teaching of Scripture or of Jesus Himself. Some notable passages are when Jesus says He is the truth (John 14:6), and the passage that says that the (Holy) Spirit of truth would guide His people to the truth (John 16:13).

The message is simple: do not rejoice in evil, but rejoice in the truth. Of course, this is much harder to live out in practice. Due to the human desire to be in control, receive praise, and have absolute power, it is easy for us to delight to see bad things happen to others. The news media receives high ratings and a large number of viewers when presenting the *bad* that is happening. The tabloids at grocery stores catch people's eyes. People want to talk about the bad that happened to others—also known as gossip. As much as we may want to acknowledge that we would not want to rejoice in evil, there is a part of us that does. That is why we need Jesus!

Christians must immerse themselves in the Scriptures and spend much time in prayer with God in order to know the truth and become one with Him. That is the way we are able to rejoice in the truth instead of rejoicing in evil. This aspect of love is difficult to keep because our hearts and minds have a tendency to desire self-gain. We need the supernatural work of God so that we can rejoice in the truth while not rejoicing in evil.

> *Christians must immerse themselves in the Scriptures and spend much time in prayer with God in order to know the truth and become one with Him. That is the way we are able to rejoice in the truth instead of rejoicing in evil.*

Love never gives up or loses faith. Love is always hopeful and endures through every circumstance. (v. 7)

Πάντα στέγει, πάντα πιστεύει, πάντα ἐλπίζει, πάντα ὑπομένει (*panta stegei, panta pistevei, panta elpizei, panta hupomenei*) are the four phrases of verse 7. *Panta* means all, always, definite, and above all. *Stegei* means to bear and endure. *Pistevei* means to believe. *Elpizei* means to hope. *Hupomenei* means to bear under and wait in perseverance. *Hupomenei* is the same word for patience that is used in 2 Peter 1:6.

Together, these phrases say that love always has faith and hope and endures in perseverance. Love believes in the best for someone, and it has faith that God can do mighty things through that person. Those who love remain over time, trusting in God that He will do what is best in the other person's life. This is why, when we pray in love for someone, we hope for the highest and the best for that person. Regardless of the person's past, Christians believe that God will do the best through them.

The apostle Paul concludes the chapter with three things that remain: faith, hope, and love (1 Corinthians 13:13). Love seems to point to patient endurance or perseverance over time. Paul is saying that faith and hope are necessary, but remaining with others over time, regardless of circumstances—to love—is the utmost and highest calling. That is why he says that things that require faith and hope, such as prophecy and speaking in tongues, will fade, *but love will last forever* (1 Corinthians 13:8).

God Is Love, and He Calls Us to Represent Him

Let us connect 1 John 4:7–8 with 1 Corinthians 13. *God is love* (1 John 4:8). In 1 Corinthians 13:4–7, the character of this love is given in greater detail. Consider the following:

- God is patient.
- God is kind.
- God is jealous (because He is God and deserves the glory).
- God is not boastful or proud.
- God is not rude. He gently guides us in ways we can follow.

- God does not demand His own way. He has given us free will to decide and act.

- God does not get offended by who we are, although He is opposed to sin and injustice.

- God does not keep a record of the evil we have done. He cleared it away through Jesus.

- God does not rejoice in injustice, but rejoices in the truth. He wants the best for us.

- God never gives up or loses faith. He is always hopeful, and He endures with us. His love endures forever, and He is now Immanuel—God with us.

As we grow in our relationship with Him, we, too, can grow in love. We must stay close to Him, especially as we seek to fulfill the highest calling—to love with the unconditional love of God.

Small-Group Reflections

1. What are the callings God has shared with you, and where do you stand in terms of action and faith on what God has planned for you?
2. How can you fulfill the highest calling from where you are today?
3. Which aspects of love would you like to improve upon, and toward whom?

Chapter Seven

Being a Disciple to Make Disciples

A Practical Guide to Executing the Great Commission through Successful Small Groups

People are searching for meaning; they can come to know God when we share God with them through our lives over time.[164]

In this final chapter, I present practical guidance on running small groups based on my limited experiences in various small groups. These are simply guidelines, as no two small groups are alike. Small groups consist of a few people with different tendencies and levels of faith. No two small groups should operate the same, nor should one be compared against another. One group that seems weak and powerless may be just the one where the members encounter God and transform the world.

The goal in this chapter is to share some beneficial discipleship principles. I hope to continue to develop these principles with other Christians, including perhaps you, as we continue to gather, learn and follow Jesus together. These principles might be a good starting point for each of us as we adapt them to our own group's needs and situations. Join with me as we help the members of the global Church grow deeper in their relationship with God. Let us begin with ourselves and our own small groups, making disciples of Jesus by first being His disciples ourselves.

Before we jump into practical guidance, consider passages in Scripture where people were called disciples. From these verses, we are able to see what it means to be a disciple of Jesus. The characteristics of a disciple are as follows:

- Called (Matthew 4:18–22)
- Believes in Jesus (John 8:31)
- Is faithful to the Word of God (John 8:31)
- Denies oneself (Matthew 16:24)
- Has the love of God (John 13:34–35)
- Humbly serves others (Mark 10:45)
- Makes other disciples (John 15:8; 2 Timothy 2:1–2)

Christians should ask themselves whether they fit these descriptions and are committed to growing as disciples of Jesus. As Christians focus on personal growth through discipleship, other disciples will naturally be made through new relationships that they form.

Basic Structure of a Small Group

The key focus of a small group is deep relationships, just as we are called to a deep relationship with God. As a result, the following four key foundational structures are being presented. The goal of small groups is to develop deep relationships through sharing lives. Therefore, it is acceptable to meet together even if members do not fit perfectly into all four structures, as long as the people are able to share their lives together with the others in the group. However,

> *The key focus of a small group is deep relationships, just as we are called to a deep relationship with God.*

the following four foundational structures are often conditions that allow for life-sharing that leads to a healthy discipleship group.

Foundational Structure 1: Individual Commitment to Growth and Life-sharing, Although Visiting is Welcome Too!

First and foremost, we must recognize that discipleship is for those who are already believers, just as worship services in churches are for them. It is okay to welcome visitors, but a group just starting out should begin with three or more people who agree and commit together to grow in discipleship. This commitment is not to say that one will not miss any future meetings or that one's schedule can never change, but it is an agreement of pursuit among three or more brothers or sisters to grow in discipleship and share their lives together to the best of their ability.

> *Discipleship is for those who are already believers. . . . Begin with three or more people who agree and commit together to grow in discipleship.*

This means that among themselves, they are agreeing to brotherhood or sisterhood; that is, they are agreeing to be there for each other, to care for and about each other, and to pray in love for each other. The members should also have in common a personal desire to grow in Christ.

After some time of gathering together among themselves, once people feel more comfortable with each other, guests may be invited. As long as the members feel they are benefitting through the relationships, they are likely to naturally invite others who are similar to them.

Since the brothers and sisters in the group are already in communication, they can give a heads-up when they intend to bring someone to their next meeting. They can welcome the new person and ensure that they feel comfortable sharing as much as they desire, while also letting them know that they are free to participate in or not participate in any activity as they deem suitable. The guests are always welcome to join in on the prayer, Bible reading, etc., but are not required to do so. They may simply observe, if that is what makes them most comfortable.

Foundational Structure 2: Proximity and Meeting in Person

With the coronavirus pandemic that has occurred across the world, many people, including those in business or in the Church, have been meeting through online video communication such as Zoom, WebEx, or Google Hangouts. Church attendance had already been in decline due to many people thinking that worship can be held by watching a sermon online. Now, with the online worship required by the pandemic, even more people might feel that this kind of worship is acceptable to God. As the world continues to turn toward individualism, where everyone is to become an island, the Church must fight to unite and come together in person whenever it is possible (see Hebrews 10:24–25).

As a result, when forming small groups, it is important to gauge proximity from one's natural location(s). A natural location is simply where the person is often located. There are generally two main locations, home and work, but depending on one's lifestyle, there can be more or less.

For example, if someone lives in a suburb outside of New York City, but works in New York City Monday through Friday, then it is reasonable to take part in a small group that meets weekly in New York City. The person may also decide to join a small group in the suburbs close to home on weekends or on evenings outside of working hours.

The reason for proximity is simple: there needs to be frequent interactions between one another. This is certainly not a hard-and-fast rule, as someone who lives an hour away may simply feel comfortable with the group, and this is acceptable as long as life-sharing can occur. However, when one begins to feel a burden to travel to meet others and gathering becomes a drag, this is a problem due to lack of proximity, which will weaken relationships. Additionally, if one person is farther away from the rest, the other members cannot comfortably visit that person, and this breaks the ability to share lives together.

> *The reason for proximity is simple: there needs to be frequent interactions between one another.*

I had a friend from high school who would show up at my doorstep without any notice. He would just peek into my bedroom window and say, "Hi, Sang! What are you doing?" When I was younger, I felt this was an invasion of my privacy. Now I realize that he was a true friend who knew me and was a person with whom I could share my deepest secrets. He stood as one of my groomsmen in my wedding, and like a true prophet and friend, he spoke honestly and fearlessly whenever I was in the wrong. We all need friends like this.

In our modern world, we are heading toward individualism, while the Church is called to community. This evolution creates two key words that Christians must be careful to manage well: privacy and globalization.

Privacy is certainly important, especially as globalization increases and devices begin to manage our identities. There ought to be greater privacy between a husband and wife than between other friends, as they are united as one as ordained by God (Genesis 2:22–24). However, there can also be friends closer than a brother

(Proverbs 18:24), where the man can confide in another brother, or a woman can confide in another sister, on things that they experience as men and women. However, as long as the individuals cling to privacy, life-sharing comes to a halt, as everyone's life is their own. Christians should not operate that way.

> *As long as the individuals cling to privacy, life-sharing comes to a halt, as everyone's life is their own. Christians should not operate that way.*

In public matters, Christians ought to be transparent and presentable enough to share their faith in and out of season (2 Timothy 4:2). In private matters, there should be a few people who can see the person, even in their weakest moments, just as Jesus allowed (Matthew 26:36–37).

For married people, this circle must occur between husband and wife first. If your marriage relationship is not good, then it is very probable that your relationship with God and your relationships with others are not good. The circle must grow to other trusted people who are of the same gender as you. Same-gender accountability is much more important when you are married because no one should possibly be a competition for your spouse, ever! Even before marriage, it is important to do this to protect your purity for your future spouse. (If you are looking to dialogue about these matters, a small group would be very helpful!)

Privacy is a growing topic, and more so as the world becomes more personalized through globalization, which requires greater security. Yet Christians must recognize that privacy can work against a God-called community, or our highest calling to love one another.

The second phenomenon that Christians must manage well is globalization. Globalization says that I can be anywhere in the world and still join you. Online churches offer this today, and many young people feel they can take part in the church through online connection. During a pandemic, while following the governmental authorities, it is good to obey and attempt to take advantage of the technology; however, this cannot be the norm. Christians are called to gather together, especially since people will want to stop doing so (Hebrews 10:25). The Church is a community of believers together as a whole, and this fellowship will persist with Jesus forever in the days to come. Individualism is rooted in each human's desire to be God, and the business world takes advantage of this fact to make more sales. Individualism isolates people from one another and from God Himself.

> *Individualism is rooted in each human's desire to be God, and the business world takes advantage of this fact to make more sales. Individualism isolates people from one another and from God Himself.*

Some people encourage making community online. In some cases, this is important, and I hope this aspect grows. One example I look forward to is being able to continue frequent family gatherings with my two children when they go to college and beyond. Online connectivity would keep us together; however, I must not settle for online gatherings over long periods of time, as it would be more precious to be able to see my children in person.

This is why proximity is important, even in the age of the internet and mobile devices. A small group must consist of brothers or sisters who are within close travelling distance of each other so that members can get together for lunch or go for a walk together as permissible. Of course, there might be times when a brother or sister travels to another country, perhaps even for an extended time. As long as it is temporary and the relationship exists and can be fostered despite the distance, it is acceptable. However, Christians should be careful about welcoming a new person who comes from a distance and wants to retain that distanced relationship.

Foundational Structure 3: Similarity in Lifestyle and in Pursuit

Is it not enough that we are united in Christ? I argued this with myself for quite some time. Requiring similarity in lifestyle and pursuit may create perceived divisions, but this is necessary and good. The reason why similarity in lifestyle and pursuit matters is because of the ability to share lives together while meeting people where they are.

Jesus met people where they were by contextualizing. He spoke to Jewish leaders differently than He spoke to the woman at the well. The apostle Paul, too, took on different roles depending on the people to whom he was ministering (1 Corinthians 9:19–23). Believers have unique callings, too, and it may benefit them to speak to people who are on similar paths. Additionally, contextualizing is beneficial in making new disciples (1 Corinthians 9:22).

Consider a scenario where there is dissimilarity in lifestyle and pursuit. A young college male joins a small group in which the other members are mothers with young children. The young college student has just gained individual responsibilities and freedom now that he is living away from his parents, while the mothers are past that phase and are heavily focused on tending to the little ones. Conversation will not correlate well, and the college student will feel estranged.

In previous sections, I shared that small groups should consist of people of the same gender. The core reason for this is because men and women are called to different things. For example, men are to be the head of the household, the buck-stops-here leader of the family who is held responsible for the family (Ephesians 5:23). As much as the wives may support them, the men must fulfill their calling from God, which likely includes his responsibilities to his family. That encouragement to press on may occur within the family, but it can be beneficial to receive encouragement from other men who are striving to do the same. Nonetheless, the separation of genders does not mean that they cannot meet once a month, or during summers, with their wives, kids, or significant others. It is wonderful for wives to connect and for kids to play together. Establishing other meetings such as golf or bowling, depending on the majority's interests, can result in wonderful times of fellowship together. As a result of these events, they can further share their lives together.

Other small groups that can form with similar lifestyles and pursuits can consist of the wives of God-fearing men. Perhaps they can be encouraged by other wives who have children and/or careers in helping their family fulfill God-given callings. Another small group might consist of Christian pastors in the region. Another group might be for Christians who are deeply into music and worship. There could be a group for single college men who want to devote themselves to God. With a similar push in their hearts, they can come together and pray to God for the power and ability to fulfill their callings. They can help one another carry out their great callings from God.

This begs the necessary question of today: Wouldn't there be separation between people of different races and cultures? The answer is both yes and no.

In the last example given, perhaps if single college women formed their own small group, they could join together with the single college men's group once every month or two to have joint fellowships. Who knows—some members might need to begin forming a new small group for newly married couples! The groups could work together, and although their focus would not be on finding a spouse, that might end up being part of it. Each group's purpose would be for discipleship, which is why they would meet with their own gender regularly to share lives together.

Today, due to recent events in the United States, there is an increased attention on racism, especially toward African Americans and the term "Black Lives Matter." Would there be a problem or a division among Christians if African Americans, Asians, and Caucasians met separately from one another? The answer is no. In fact, it could be better at times.

Let me explain. African Americans might live in close proximity to other African Americans. African Americans might also best relate to other African Americans—perhaps even more so if they immigrated to America in their adult age. The same is probably true with Asians and people of all other cultures. As a result, it is more important to connect with people who can support one another from where they are. The greatest importance in a small group is whether or not the members are able to comfortably share their lives with each other.

Now let's suppose that when a Caucasian group comes together for a meeting, one or more of the members share that they feel led to do something about the racism against Blacks in America. They can reach out to an African American small group near them and ask if they would be willing to partner together, or perhaps simply hold joint meetings together so that they can collectively work on this and serve Christ together. And of course, a small group can also easily be formed with members of different cultures and backgrounds if they live in close proximity to each other and have similar interests and/or pursuits.

Additionally, I can say with great confidence that the brothers who form the Christian Businessmen small group in NYC come from all kinds of cultures and backgrounds. They have different kinds of education, work experiences, and financial situations, but one who has much does not have too much, nor does a person who has little have too little. It has been just enough (this is the message of Exodus 16:18, repeated again in the context of giving in 2 Corinthians 8:12–15). Our many conversations together that enable us to move forward as a collective whole demonstrate that such culturally diverse groups are able to be fruitful.

The only question that remains for the Christians in small groups is: Are you able to share your lives together? This may be a question directed to individuals who may feel estranged, or to the group as a whole if they are unable to tolerate the differences in lifestyles and pursuits of the members in the group.

However, as long as the members are able to connect and are comfortable sharing their lives together, the requirement for similarity is less relevant. For example, perhaps in a group of male Christian attorneys, a musician is in their midst. If the musician and the attorneys are able to connect in conversations and relationships and are not burdened by the differences, similarity is no longer a requirement. On the other hand, if the musician is focused on the pursuit of music while the attorneys recognize a different calling for them, then that may be a hindrance in going deeper in relationship. Perhaps, depending on the strength and longevity of the group, the solution is not to dissolve the group, but instead to invite others to the group so that the one group can split into two where the members of each group can relate better to one another.

Lastly, consider how a fugitive gathered people together to form a brotherhood among others like him, building allegiance and support, even until he became a king, keeping those loyal brothers near him even when he was the king. First Samuel 22:1–2 says that David began to gather with similar people, *men who were in trouble or in debt or who were just discontented.* David formed a brotherhood with such men at this phase of his life and had recognition from about four hundred men. In such a relationship, these four hundred men would probably follow each other in different pursuits because they trusted each other. In this story, they trusted David and followed him. These are likely the people David placed as his kingdom officials because of his trust in them as well.

Similarities can lead to small groups operating together for the kingdom of God. This can happen because of the similarities that God may have placed in their life's circumstances or pursuits. Consider also the small groups covered in chapter 5 that accomplished great results; those small groups formed because of their similar passion and calling. In David's story, the group that began with four hundred men continued to grow in number. The same will happen in small groups, as members who meet in small numbers interact with others who know them, and so forth.

Similarities allow for life-sharing, and that is where the depth of love and direction, both individually and collectively, can be found so that we can seek to fulfill the calling that God has for us.

> *Similarities allow for life-sharing, and that is where the depth of love and direction, both individually and collectively, can be found so that we can seek to fulfill the calling that God has for us.*

Foundational Structure 4: Frequent Meetings Over Time—In Groups and as Individuals

> They worshiped together at the Temple each day, met in homes for the Lord's Supper, and shared their meals with great joy and generosity.
>
> Acts 2:46

Frequently—that is the answer to how often small groups should meet.

It is true that back in Jesus's day, people lived close to each other and were able to meet daily (and often multiple times a day!), whereas today, people who have gotten to know each other live and work much farther away from each other, making this difficult. That is why Christians in close proximity to each other should form their own groups whenever possible. Ideally, the members should be close enough so that they can drop by another person's work or home with short notice. This is what it means to share lives together.

> *Frequently—that is the answer to how often small groups should meet.... The frequent interactions of the group enable the growth in relationship, accountability, and discipleship.*

It is important to plan for frequent meetings. In my experience, once a week is necessary. The frequent interactions of the group enable the growth in relationship, accountability, and discipleship. The weekly meetings also allow busy individuals to block the time, prioritizing the small-group meeting.

The meetings may certainly be every two to four weeks, but that tends to cause lags in relationship building, and since so much can happen during that time, members can end up talking at a superficial level when they come together for a short gathering. Even though some members recognize the need for depth and seek to provide and receive genuine conversation, that may not happen simply because of time constraints. Out of courtesy to allow everyone to speak, members might only speak at a surface level, and the deeper conversation might be left for another time—which means it would probably not happen.

In addition to weekly meetings, the members should call each other to meet for lunch, exercise, sports, or even to visit their workplace in order to spend individual time together. The goal is not to make the meetings obligatory and forced, but to develop deeper relationships with each other as they grow in discipleship together.

What Are the Results That May Occur in a Small Group Meeting?

This can be summed up in three words: Nothing. Something. Everything.

Nothing

The group meets even in the midst of *nothing*; that is, the group meets even if nothing changes in one's circumstances or there is nothing new to talk about. The members can simply get together, go through a planned activity (see the next section for suggested content for small-group meetings), and pray for one another. It may seem as if nothing is happening, but the members of the group recognize it as part of the process.

Something

The goal of each meeting is to share lives together. This may mean that when there is an hour-and-a-half meeting and activity planned, and one member shows up with a serious situation or question, then the conversation of the entire meeting might be solely around that. The needs of the members take higher priority over generally planned activities. Allow God to take control. He may bring that *something*.

The group should often have a general plan of what to cover that the members can go through together, such as a group devotional, a chapter of the Bible, or a Christian book on a topic of interest. The plan would be to go through that material during the meeting, but it would take second place to allowing the members to share their lives. Some examples would be new prayer requests, successes or failures regarding things discussed in past meetings, or new direction from God. Other possible plans might include building a new plan together for group activities for future meetings. The group together operates organically and makes decisions as a group to best enable the sharing of lives, including that of family, work/business, and anything else that is important to them. Then they can lift them up in prayer to God. Leave it to God and trust Him to guide the meetings and produce the results. He will bring that something.

Everything

Through these gatherings, life transformations may occur. Individuals may come to recognize how far they have turned away from God, or they realize that a certain sin is preventing them from going forward in fulfilling their great calling. The members can bring up questions about major decisions in their lives, and they can pray together and ask God for insight.

Members experience God together and see Him bring about breakthroughs. Healings can happen. Miracles can occur. They happen in the context of relationships, and the brothers and sisters will be there when these things happen—and during the aftermath as well. Life is transformed and renewed, and new direction is established. God becomes their *everything* as He changes *everything*.

During the years of knowing each other, they can see each other through, encouraging each other when they need it because they know what obstacles the person has already overcome in their lives. God may work in them and through them over a long period of time, and the trusted brothers and sisters can be with them along the way.

What Should Be Done In Small-Group Gatherings?

> *All the believers devoted themselves to the apostles' teaching, and to fellowship, and to sharing in meals (including the Lord's Supper), and to prayer.*
>
> Acts 2:42

Four key components of a successful small group are listed in the verse above. They are:

- Study/devotion to the Word of God
- Fellowship, or spending unrushed time together
- Eating together
- Prayer

It is important to recognize that the above four things do not need to occur at every meeting, but the members can decide together how to best accomplish this. This can mean dedicating one meeting each month to prayer, while other meetings might consist of reading a devotional and eating together. Every now and then, the members might go out and watch a movie, go bowling, or have a party at a member's house in which family and friends are invited. All of this can occur over time.

Where Should We Meet for Small Groups?

Strive to meet at a person's home or, for business owners or professionals who may have space to meet, at a workplace. Rotate locations by members if logistically possible. This serves two purposes: (1) The group meeting will be unrushed as opposed to meeting in cafés and restaurants where customers are expected to leave once the meal/drink is finished. 2) It is more welcoming and lives are better shared as the host opens their homes/businesses to others.

When either of these options are not available, aim for public places such as cafés and restaurants, or possibly outdoor parks where the recurring unrushed meeting might be possible.

Characteristics of Strong Small Groups

- *Self-directed.* There should generally be no external influence or authority to establish rules on how the small group functions. This means that small groups are not as successful when they are under the direction or authority of a church or a pastor. The members of the small group are people who love God and desire to grow in their faith. They should seek to follow God as He leads them.

    At times, only as a decision of the members of the small group, they may request a pastor to guide them, perhaps as they are starting out; however, the choice belongs to the members of the small group to direct such decisions and grow as they see fit.

- *Frequent communication between members,* often using a mobile group-chat feature. Individuals can share news about their activities, prayer requests as they come up, or encouraging words or media that encouraged them. This can provide a venue for engagement and involvement of all the members, even outside the weekly meeting.

- *Daily Bible readings and sharing a favorite verse.* The small group would pick a book of the Bible to start from, reading one chapter each day and sharing one verse from that reading in a group chat as used above. As a result of each person sharing, the members are encouraged to read the Bible on their own and engage with the group. Additionally, this allows members to share their thoughts about the verse or ask questions to allow for further engagement. If any major topic comes up, the group may decide to go deeper when they get together.

- *Coordinator or leader.* In some sense, the word *coordinator* fits well because a strong small group is one in which everyone is engaged. As brothers/sisters who are equals, they ought to make decisions together for anything, whether plans for weekly meetings, future activities, decisions to shift the focus, etc.

    However, the word *leader* may also be used because this person would be the one to set up the administrative components, such as scheduling the meeting, which may include contacting others, securing methods and/or locations to meet, etc. Additionally, as busyness takes over many Christians' lives, the coordinator may need to go outside of administrative boundaries to reach out to the person as a spiritual leader/encourager, helping them draw back to

Christ. This kind of leadership is especially important while the group is forming and learning to work together.

The coordinator or leader should provide ample communication. This allows for members to engage and feel connected to the group's activities.

The coordinator or leader should pray, and should do so often. Such a person can lead others to trust in God more regarding life's circumstances and decisions. All members should follow suit, but it often begins with the urging and encouragement of one or two people who make this the culture of the group.

- *Small group size.* In keeping the relationships as the priority, the groups cannot be too big for an extended time. The ideal size should be eight, with a minimum of three and a maximum of twelve. I said "extended time" because there may be times when we invite others and have a group of fifteen or twenty. That's okay, as long as it does not become the norm. After some of these exception meetings, a regular-sized small-group meeting must take place so that the members can get back to speaking their minds and sharing their lives.

- *Welcome variations.* The key benefit of small groups is that they are small and can move relatively quickly, much like the agility of business start-ups compared to that of an established business. As a practical example, when enough members announce that they cannot make the next meeting, the two, three, or four who are available might go out to eat at a nice restaurant instead of holding a regular meeting. Instead of meeting at a restaurant, some other activities could be welcome too. This is how we put life-sharing first. Note that those hours were not spent in worship or reading the Bible, even though that is certainly something that can be done.

- *Meet weekly.* As mentioned earlier, a week seems to be the best interval for formal small-group meetings. This allows for busy people to schedule and remember the time for the meetings. Additionally, it provides a short enough interval so members can catch up with any changes that occurred during that short time. It also is not so long that members who miss the meeting cannot catch up the following week. When members miss too many meetings, they will begin to feel estranged from the group. Meeting intervals that go beyond a week tend to have the negative impacts that were mentioned earlier, including difficulty in scheduling, as well as being forced to speak at a surface level or without depth out of courtesy for each other.

- *Same gender.* This allows for greater intimacy without fear of lustful attraction, and it promotes faithful purity toward their spouse or future spouse. This is of utmost importance in a small-group setting, where there may be times when only two members would connect and go in depth about things that are most private and important to them. As relationships deepen and conversations occur, there may be topics reserved for close friends or spouses. Sharing with anyone who may even provide a perception of distrust between spouses, possibly even causing hints of jealousy, will estrange marriages and relationships within small groups. As men, we must protect our wives by leaving no doubt that we love our spouse more than anyone else on earth.

    Additionally, this keeps the sacred unity of marriage, even for a person who is not yet married. It allows the person to keep purity of heart so that there is no regret by thinking back to times when deepest secrets were shared with someone other than the spouse, especially one with whom they should not have ties as strong as love for the spouse. Keeping away from opposite genders is such an important rule that within pastoral circles, the older pastors often teach younger pastors to never even get in a car with someone of the opposite gender, usually for their own sake to protect themselves against temptation and rumors.

Small groups that do not keep genders separate may be able to worship and pray together, but the depth of the relationship will likely be limited. If a certain line is crossed in a small group made up of both genders, there may be relational conflicts and/or regrets, perhaps leading to further estrangement from one another.

- *A place to come and see.* A small group is successful when it is an open and welcoming environment for Christians and for not-yet-Christians to come and simply observe. This is what happened when the Samaritan woman met Jesus and started telling everyone about her experience. They needed to come and see and experience Him for themselves. When they did, they came to truly believe (John 4:42). The same occurred with Nathaniel when Phillip invited him to come and see (John 1:45–46).

Possible Content for Small-Group Meetings

I remember leading Bible studies many years ago. I worked hard to prepare the study materials. The material I had prepared took longer to get through than the hour allocated for the meeting. I requested members to stay "just another thirty minutes." Some people fidgeted, while others had to leave to make their next appointments. Then we had to make the decision to either continue the study at our next meeting or start the next agreed-upon topic to move things along. It seemed as if I spent more of the group's time, energy, and focus on the administrative and logistic aspects than upon the message itself. The members probably did not remember much of the message since they were instead likely thinking about the meeting running long! This seems to be the case when the study takes priority over the relationships or the sharing of lives together.

The content is not the main focus for small-group meetings, but it is a helpful resource to enable the greater focus, which is the sharing of lives. More important than what a single person has prepared are the questions and topics of concern from the members, including what has been happening in their lives, such as matters of family, work, and interactions with others. As a result, content is always considered to be a backup, though it is important for the members to agree on what content, topic, and material they want to use.

For example, in certain small groups, I have used *Our Daily Bread* daily devotionals. I provided a printout of the devotion of the day for each member. We would start on the devotional only if there was time left after the initial formalities and sharing.

In another small group that consisted of Christian businessmen, material from the Christian Business Men's Connection (CBMC), called "Monday Manna," was used. In other groups, we selected a specific chapter or passage of the Bible.

Here is an example of what a small-group meeting looks like: The small-group meeting begins with people trickling in and just talking comfortably until a quorum is formed. Then one person prays for the meal, and we continue our conversations as we eat together.

Naturally, the topic remains on individuals and whatever may be on our minds. If there is any administrative information that needs to be shared, it is shared then as well. If anyone needs special attention, prayer, or dialogue about a certain topic, the group stays focused on that; however, if the conversations have stalled, the group goes on to the backup content.

The backup content should be thought-provoking and relevant to the members. It can include topics about fatherhood, leadership, working, or anything else that would lead the group to talk in depth of their experiences in life. The group would read through the material together, perhaps taking turns reading a paragraph at a time, and then they would discuss any questions listed in the resource, or they could share what they got out of the message they have read. Some other ideas would be to watch a sermon together, perhaps one that connects with the similarities of the members; to discuss current events and relate them to proper mindsets or actions in light of Scripture; or even to have a strict Scripture reading with or without dialogue between the sections of Scripture.

The content should generally require little or no preparation, because if it required preparation, it would put a burden on the person leading it. It could even lead to a sermon, which does not belong in a small-group meeting. Rather, it should be something members can work on during their time together to explore and share together as they are led.

The members can reserve the last twenty minutes or so of the meeting for prayer requests and to spend time praying for each other. This is optional, just as other components of the meeting are, and the special time of group prayer can certainly be held at other times as the members feel the need for it.

As an example, a small group of businessmen in NYC decided to have a separate prayer meeting during the Coronavirus pandemic specifically to pray for each of the brothers, along with other topics that God might bring to their attention. The membership of the small group should decide together the components of their meetings based on how God leads them.

The above is just an example of a basic meeting. Other meetings may involve going out to play golf or having a bigger gathering, inviting all family members to someone's house. Life-sharing is key to the meetings, and as a result, all aspects of a person's life, including family, work, and other interests, must be affected as a result of God transforming lives through discipleship.

> *Life-sharing is key to the meetings, and as a result, all aspects of a person's life, including family, work, and other interests, must be affected as a result of God transforming lives through discipleship.*

The Importance of Eating Together (An Eating Ministry!)

Special mention must be made about this important aspect of discipleship. Some people jest that they have an eating ministry, but that is nothing to joke about since it truly is a key aspect of ministry!

Eating together is one of the key aspects of sharing lives together. It is sad to see that some churches, especially more established and larger ones, do not leave time for this since it allows for greater fellowship and sharing of love among one another. In such churches, the members simply sit for the service and then leave. Members do not know each other. Without fellowship, I am afraid that churches are becoming more of a religion for people who seek to meet religious requirements.

Fellowship is key to coming together in community. Acts 2:42 specifically says that the members broke bread together. Acts 2:46 repeats

> *Eating together should be part of church services, as well as a requirement for all small groups.*

this, as well as other passages such as Acts 20:7. Jesus, too, ate with sinners (Matthew 11:19). When Jesus fed the five thousand and the four thousand, it implied that He provided an environment for fellowship and that eating together was important (Matthew 14:13–21; Matthew 15:32–38). Eating together should be part of church services, as well as a requirement for all small groups. Note that this is one deficiency of online gatherings.

Why is eating together so important? Eating together recognizes that whether we are Black, Asian, or Hispanic, we all need food and other provisions from God. It levels us to say that one person is not better than anyone else, regardless of class or other societal divisions. It is to say that we are all alike and that we are all the same in the eyes of God—we are all His children.

Consider David inviting Mephibosheth to his dining table (2 Samuel 9:10). Even though David was the king, he welcomed someone who was not of his class to partake in fellowship with him. This same David, as he grew in deeper relationship with God, recognized that God prepared and invited him to dine with Him, even though he was just a human (Psalm 23:5). This also teaches Christians who have been called to a higher status or have more resources to provide for and welcome those who may be blessed in other ways (Matthew 25:35–40).

In sharing life together, Jesus probably shared many meals together with His disciples. One of the most pronounced meals they had together is called the Last Supper (Matthew 26:20–30). It is called the "last" because there were many other occasions when they ate together. As disciples of Jesus, we, too, should practice eating together and allowing the conversation to flow freely without consideration of race, status, gender, or other societal divisions. And don't forget to pray together before eating. This little act brings the members together and also focuses the thanks to God at the onset of the meeting.

How Does Power Evangelism Fit Into Small-Group Discipleship?

Discussion about discipleship, which includes evangelism and life-on-life sharing, cannot be concluded without discussing healing, miracles, and raising the dead. The reason is simple: Jesus lived His life on earth as an example for us to follow (1 Corinthians 11:1; Ephesians 5:1–2; 1 John 2:6), and His life included both small-group discipleship *and* healings, deliverances, and miracles.

Jesus and His disciples performed healings, deliverances, and miracles for two reasons: (1) to show God's love for the people, and (2) to demonstrate the power of God. As a result of these miracles, people came to know God. Evangelism by demonstrating miracles of God is called "power evangelism" by John Wimber.[165] Demonstrating the love of God and showing God's power through healings and miracles is certainly something that all Christians must acknowledge and should be able to put into practice; however, this in itself is not evangelism.

Recall that *evangelism* is a word that is used loosely to point to the Great Commission, which is actually a call to make disciples.[166] Signs and wonders may

> *Signs and wonders may initiate a person experiencing God and feeling His love, but that by itself will not form a disciple.*

initiate a person in experiencing God and feeling His love, but that by itself will not form a disciple. Disciples are followers of Jesus who are committed to *continued life-on-life growth over time with others*. A person experiencing a miracle who does not connect with other believers with a commitment to share lives and grow with others over time may only draw close to God temporarily. This is what the seeds that fell on rocky soil represent (Matthew 13:20–21).

That is why John tells us that people did not believe in Jesus, despite the miracles they saw (John 12:37–41). People followed Jesus seeking and desiring miracles, but even with all those miracles, their faith in God did not grow. This is similar to having a dire prayer request. "If I only had that person as my husband (or wife)," "If I could bear just one child," or "If I could just have five thousand dollars"—when such prayer requests are granted, the person may receive it with great joy and may even make rash commitments, but their faith may soon wander. (See Ecclesiastes 5:1–7 for teachings on vain worship, including making rash commitments that do not last.) Abraham, David, and all the spiritual heroes of the past were required to go through a faith journey over a period of time in order to grow in faith. *Power evangelism* by itself does not produce the disciple that is commanded in the Great Commission.

Additionally, there were clear examples shared through Jesus's life. In John 6, people were following Jesus, seeking even more miracles (John 6:2, 24, 30), for they had already seen many healings (John 6:2) and other miracles, such as being fed much with little (John 6:14, 26). When Jesus taught them His truth and asked them to have faith

> *When Jesus taught them His truth and asked them to have faith in God, many people, including those who had seen miracles and healings, left Jesus. However, the people who remained were those with whom Jesus had life-on-life discipleship relationships.*

in God, many people, including those who had seen miracles and healings, left Jesus (John 6:66). However, the people who remained were those with whom Jesus had life-on-life discipleship relationships (John 6:68–69).

It is clear throughout the life of Jesus and the apostles that healings and miracles, including raising the dead, were indispensably important in demonstrating the love of God and showing God. Love is the source of that power, and that love is who God is (1 John 4:7–21).

Just as the crowd sought the power that Jesus demonstrated for their own use and pride (John 6:28), some may try to imitate this power and claim to do these things in the name of Jesus (Matthew 24). Many of those people will believe they are Christians because of these miracles, but Jesus rebukes them (Matthew 7:21–23). Perhaps the proper way to identify the validity and source of this power is to see if these people come in the *love of Jesus Christ*. Are they seeking a relationship, or are they simply seeking a show of power for their own gain? Love practiced in small groups is necessary to make true disciples.

> *Are they seeking a relationship, or are they simply seeking a show of power for their own gain? Love practiced in small groups is necessary to make true disciples.*

Even when Jesus demonstrated the power of God, He practiced *love with God and His disciples*. For example, in Matthew 26, Jesus ate with His disciples, and then went on to pray with a few of them. This could be Jesus inviting others to pray for Him regarding His dire prayer request (Matthew 26:39). In other

> *Even when Jesus demonstrated the power of God, He practiced love with God and His disciples.*

sections of the Gospels, we see Jesus spending time with God. For example, we see in Luke 5:15–16, that when the crowds came to Jesus for healing, He withdrew to spend time with God. Jesus also spent time with His disciples (e.g., Luke 8:1).

Additionally, as mentioned in chapter 5, it is prayer, relationship with God, and being together with other believers in small groups that resulted in great power. *Love* must take precedence. Christians ought to desire and take part in small groups of like-minded believers and expect great things from God *together*. *The kingdom of God is not just a lot of talk; it is living by God's power* (1 Corinthians 4:20).

The Proper Length of Small-Group Meetings

The proper length of weekly meetings is to be determined by the group jointly. In my experience, some successful meetings were set to one hour during lunchtimes as the coordinator was careful to watch the time and keep the team on track. Some more successful meetings began at a specific time, such as 7:00 p.m., while the ending time was left open. The meetings sometimes ended at 9:00 p.m., while at other times they went past 11:00 p.m. Depending on the topic at hand and how the meeting flowed, the brothers kept going, while some who had time constraints were free to leave. Often when meetings were capped at about two hours, the members felt that more time was needed.

In the minds of the members, *unrushed time* is very important. Living in a business-driven world, Christians may consider a small-group meeting to be like a business meeting, and that is where the relationship aspect will fall short. Business meetings often have goals in mind, and the meeting's purpose is to most efficiently accomplish that goal. For example, it may be a status meeting where the goal is to cover all statuses in the most effective way possible.

> *Living in a business-driven world, Christians may consider a small-group meeting to be like a business meeting, and that is where the relationship aspect will fall short. . . . Efficiency is not the goal, but the goal is to welcome one another to each other's lives and share their lives together.*

A small-group meeting is focused on discipleship, or relationships and growth through these relationships. Efficiency is not the goal, but the goal is to welcome one another to each other's lives and share their lives together. As a result, the members must commit to unrushed time when together, and that should dictate what a normal length of the meeting ought to be.

Special Small Groups—Family

Fathers are called to lead and disciple their families to Christ. In the absence of a father, the second-in-command—the mother—must carry on in this role. Family is a core, God-ordained small group. As a result, the same discipleship is necessary among family members. Even when children are older, your families will likely have the same depth of relationship with each other that you have with God.

How Many Small Groups Should I Join?

One.

Let me elaborate. A small group forms a brotherhood or sisterhood. When people belong to multiple small groups, they are divided and may even begin to compare the groups to each other. (Perhaps this is similar to people who feel that they belong to multiple churches, when in reality they truly belong to none.)

Christians should devote themselves to one small group and should work to operate together with the members of that small group. For example, if someone feels an urge in their heart to take action due to a recent tragedy that occurred to some African Americans in the United States, that person should share that with the group and attempt to plan out actions together, or at least the group members should agree to pray for that person as he or she operates alone or with other groups.

There are some exceptions, though. Depending on your life's calling, there could be two different kinds of people to whom God has called you. It is acceptable to take part in another small group as long as you are able to share lives with both groups and are able to welcome members of both groups into your life. You might also be able to be in two small groups if your church has a small group, but you feel that a more specialized small group is more closely aligned with your calling and would be beneficial.

Three small groups would be a stretch, and you may wish to question your own motives if you want to join three groups.

There is another small group that I have not counted in my suggestions above—family small groups. If you are a father or a single mother, this is one group you should create while your children are young. Aim for daily devotionals together, again with the primary goal of relationship building. Become a united family, even though many families in this world are in need of mending. Represent the depth and unity of Christ and the Church through your God-ordained families.

> *If you are a father or a single mother, this is one group you should create while your children are young. Aim for daily devotionals together, again with primary goal of relationship building. . . . Represent the depth and unity of Christ and the Church through your God-ordained families.*

Administrative Stuff: When Should I Start a New Small Group? When Should We Disband Our Small Group? How Do We Split?

Small groups should start when three or more members have come together in commitment for the sake of discipleship. Small groups may disband if members lose their commitment and lose interest.

When a group is consistently attended by only two people, it may make sense to simply join another small group that is nearby and has similar interests. When the group is made up of three people who are all still committed, that is sufficient to keep the group going. The three people may even consider inviting others to the group.

There is a special topic of disbanding when too many members are consistently present in small groups. The term would be "splitting." When there are ten or more members consistently in the small group, the members should begin to think of splitting the group to encourage greater engagement and life-sharing.

Details of the split must be discussed by the small-group members, and they must support the *disbanding group*. The variations that the different members bring should be considered, along with the best ways to split the group.

For example, a group might have begun with three people who lived near each other who invited friends from far away. Now there are ten people in total, but four of them come from farther away. If the four have grown sufficiently in discipleship and are willing to meet on their own, they can form another group closer to where they live, disbanding from the six members who would remain.

Another method to disband would be based upon variations in interests. In a previous example, I mentioned a small group where there was one professional musician in the midst of attorneys. If a few other musicians have joined the group, or if some of the attorneys are also involved in or have an interest in music ministries, the people who have an interest in music ministries can form another group, allowing the Christian attorneys to continue to build their relationships while also welcoming others like them.

Regardless of the rationale for how the split occurs, the sending group must always support those who have formed the new group. They ought to occasionally check in with the new group, and should also welcome the new group to meet with them, perhaps once a month, so they can remain in relationship. The same goes for the newly formed group in relation to supporting the parent group that they have left.

What a Small Group Is Not

Due to many misperceptions of how Jesus and His disciples practiced a small discipleship group, this section explains what a small group is not. You can also use this list to gauge whether or not your church practices small groups as Jesus taught. A small group is NOT:

- *A mass or a group that extends to more than twelve people.* The group is intentionally small so that lives can be shared. Having too many people prevents the ability of everyone to engage. Discipleship is not a passive event simply following the instructions of others. It must impact and touch every part of life, especially as relationships deepen. Additionally, the number of people must be limited so that when not-yet-Christians are invited, they are given the ability to engage and ask questions.

- *A worship service.* There is certainly a time for worship, and the small group may also spend time in worship, but the purpose of the small group is life-sharing. Some key aspects of a worship service that the small-group members must be mindful of are preaching sermons and an extended time of praise. A time of praise is always welcome, but spending too much time in this can lead to less time and focus on life-sharing.

- *A place for sermons by the educated (or positional) few*, where one or two people in position (pastors) give unilateral messages. In a small group, all members are to be involved and engaged. A presentation by a brother or sister of a group is good if the situation calls for it, and it might even be enjoyable and engaging when all members take part in preparing their own biblical message or Bible study. The members can attempt this if they have a moderate-to-good knowledge of Scripture. It might help if the small group is connected to a pastor or two who can help provide answers when the members are unable to resolve a theological concern.

- *A one-person show.* Work together so that one or two people do not dominate the meetings. It is acceptable to have one person handle logistics and administrative functions such as sending email reminders and coordinating the next meeting location, but the members must be able to decide together.

- *Established as an extension of administrative church work.* Certain churches divide members into small groups with the intent of sharing church administrative duties. For example, one men's group might wash dishes after fellowship. Though it is certainly possible for small groups within a church to take on administrative tasks, it must be made clear to the small-group members that the focus of the small group is discipleship. Otherwise, the members will not draw close to one another in deep fellowship, but will instead see work as the function of the group. Additionally, if this is the only fellowship that they experience within the church, the members may begin to see their identity as Christians by their work and accomplishments of administrative tasks.

- *Always associated with a local church.* Even though small groups are encouraged to be used in local church settings, they may exist outside of the local church. For example, CBMC, YWAM, CRU, IHOP, and even Prayer Tents are sodalities that do not operate within the core function of local churches (modalities). Local church leadership should encourage members to take part in small groups outside of their church since they can benefit from sharing their lives with others like them. For example, small groups in local churches might establish their groups by location or age. However, when someone recognizes their call in the marketplace or in worldwide missions, they may benefit from sharing life with others who have a similar calling and pursuit.

How to Evangelize

Make disciples. We do this by first being a disciple of Jesus ourselves. Out of the overflow of deep relationships built through discipleship, we will naturally be an influence to not-yet-Christians in our midst.

Remember to retain contextualization in your small groups. Welcome people who can relate to you, and help them feel comfortable in the midst of believers who are similar to them.

Collectively and individually, ask God about potential members to invite, and be on the alert for them. Pray for them as you invite them to the gatherings.

Whenever a new member joins, introduce everyone and make the new person feel as comfortable as possible. Take unrushed time to get to know the person, and allow the new member to take time to get to know you.

Introduce the gospel as time and environment allow. Help the new person feel at home, and allow them to participate at their comfort level, encouraging them to interact, share, and ask questions if they desire.

Through dialogues and friendships, welcome the person to faith as God allows. In the end, it will be the lives and interactions of the members of the small group that will show and attract people to God.

The Role of Pastors in Small Groups

> *Timothy, my dear son, be strong through the grace that God gives you in Christ Jesus. You have heard me teach things that have been confirmed by many reliable witnesses. Now teach these truths to other*

trustworthy people who will be able to pass them on to others.

2 Timothy 2:1–2

The role of a pastor (shepherd) is to lead Christians to do the ministry of Christ. You would be failing as a pastor if your main work is to work with individuals in handling their life's affairs while the Christians in your care are unable to minister where God has placed them.

> *You would be failing as a pastor if your main work is to work with individuals in handling their life's affairs while the Christians in your care are unable to minister where God has placed them.*

There is a very important reason why I write this section. Due to the declining church membership in many first-world countries, the role of the pastor has shifted in ways that do not please God. I remember asking a pastor, "If your church ceased to exist today, would anyone in the community know or even care?" I was basically asking if he believed that his church had any impact in the community. The response was something to the extent of, "Probably not, but God asks us to care for those whom God has given to be under our care. We cannot be mindful of others in the neighborhood." Though the response was a bit discouraging and perhaps revealed how some pastors are ignorant about their neighbors, there is some truth to this statement. Pastors *should care for those whom God places under their care*, but as the local

> *The sad truth is that many pastors are looking inwardly and are often seeking to maintain their current membership. Their focus is on sermons that excite people, and their interest remains inside the four walls of their church.*

church that represents the Church as a whole, its members must be equipped to be the salt and light of the world, including in their neighborhood and wherever else they may be. The sad truth is that many pastors are looking inwardly and are often seeking to maintain their current membership. Their focus is on sermons that excite people, and their interest remains inside the four walls of their church.

Additionally, many pastors tend to be busy. Ask anyone around them why they believe this is so, and they will say they have no clue. When we observe what these pastors do, we see that they might be busy in their private quarters trying to prepare a good sermon, and at times they are doing Christian works such as helping the members in need, driving them around, taking them to hospital/doctor appointments, and perhaps translating for them when language is a barrier. These are good things that Christians ought to do, but if the pastor does all this and has no time for some others who may need his help, then the pastor has failed and the church has failed.

Pastors must go beyond simply being good Christians on their own and leading others who believe in Jesus. The most prominent characteristic of a pastor must be availability. This means that anyone who comes to the pastor is welcome and can receive the love of Christ from him. That is modeling Jesus; however, most pastors report that they are too busy.

Pastors, as leaders of churches, must be the first to model availability. This cannot be done if he is doing all the work of helping others while no one can learn from him. A pastor's sermons will have no impact unless the people see the pastor model Christ in their

> A pastor's sermons will have no impact unless the people see the pastor model Christ in their midst.

midst. It would be better for a pastor to spend less time preparing sermons and instead spend that time with other members of the church, truly getting to know them so that he can speak words of life in ways that might impact them.

In my study in 2018–2019 regarding whether small groups are able to welcome not-yet-believers, two small groups were formed: one was a group of businessmen who loved Jesus and were laymen in their local churches; the other was a group of seminary-studied church leaders, including some who had been ordained as pastors. The result? The church leadership group was unable to invite any not-yet-Christians to their meetings, and they disbanded rather quickly. The Christian businessmen welcomed six not-yet-Christians, three of whom stayed in touch and participated in the meetings, even after the study was completed.

Why are pastors often so busy? I believe it may be because they, too, have succumbed to the trends and views of the world. They see their role as a job in which they must be kept busy during their work hours, because if they are not, they may need another job. So they work hard at whatever they know to do, including helping church members, with some pastors even working hard to appease members in order to maintain the church membership (see Galatians 1:10). Being a pastor was never meant to be a job. It is a calling.

> *Being a pastor was never meant to be a job. It is a calling.*

If pastors try to fulfill their role by treating it as a job rather than a calling, where their role, as defined by the world's trend, is to help those in need and to go "evangelize," then members will

> *If pastors try to fulfill their role by treating it as a job rather than a calling, where their role, as defined by the world's trend, is to help those in need and to go "evangelize," then members will likewise focus on their roles as engineers, doctors, or whatever their professions may be, following the ways of their spiritual leader—who happens to be blind.*

likewise focus on their roles as engineers, doctors, or whatever their professions may be, following the ways of their spiritual leader—who happens to be blind (Matthew 15:14). Neither the pastors nor the members who look up to the pastors would be doing the work of God; instead, they would be living no differently than the rest of the world. This is not why Jesus died and left us with a great calling.

The pastor's role is to enable other Christians to minister. If you are a pastor, enable the men and women in your church to effectively minister among their families and in their workplaces. Teach them to be role models in the way they live so that others will see Christ through them. Teach them to form relationships with those they meet. Enable them to fulfill their calling as you pursue yours. Pray for them individually as you get to know each person deeply. You cannot pray for anyone deeply without having a relationship with them. Teach your congregation to hold deep relationships with one another, while you do the same with a select few, as Jesus did (Luke 6:12–16).

Finally, let go of what you might have thought your role was, but instead teach your members to do the things that you were taught. This includes preparing sermons and leading Bible studies, sharing their testimonies, administering the Lord's Supper, blessing others, and praying for them. Enable your congregation to practice among one another so that they can go out into the world and welcome not-yet-Christians. Your congregation may minister to them better than you are able to because they already have a relationship with them.

> *Your congregation may minister to them better than you may be able to because they already have a relationship with them.*

For Christians who are under the care of a shepherd-pastor, remember that it is your role as a Christian to be a disciple of Jesus. Your role is to bring people to Christ and help others who are in need as you continue to grow as a disciple of Jesus. Support your spiritual leaders by caring for their needs and following their guidance (Hebrews 13:17). Be impactful in your community, both where your church is and wherever else you might go, including your home and work. You can do this by being different from the rest of the world; that is, be available, as Jesus always is for you. Your love, developed through discipleship, is what not-yet-Christians will see, and that is how they will come to know Jesus (John 13:34–35).

The Goal of Every Meeting

A small group should have one goal, and that is to bring our lives and pursuits together to Jesus. This occurs through life-sharing and recognizing the joys and struggles that each individual member experiences. As members get to know one another, they are able to pray more deeply and more meaningfully for one another. Additionally, as the Lord speaks to each person, they are able to share that with the other brothers or sisters to encourage them to keep going.

> *As members get to know one another, they are able to pray more deeply and more meaningfully for one another.*

The same is true regarding pursuits of life. Many people outside the Church may pursue career goals or other paths that might be taught in schools. Christians have a different calling, which is often much greater than we can imagine (Ephesians 3:20). That is why we need to depend on God and trust Him to fulfill His great calling for our lives.

> *Christians have a different calling, which is often much greater than we can imagine. That is why we need to depend on God and trust Him to fulfill His great calling for our lives.*

Our callings may be so unique that when discussed with people who do not know God, they may be dismissed or ridiculed. For that reason, many Christians have stopped pursuing the calling that

> *They can pray for each other and encourage one another to keep going. They can effectively bring their pursuits to Jesus together and ask God to make something of them.*

God has placed on their lives. This is where Christians of similar pursuits come in. They can pray for each other and encourage one another to keep going. They can effectively bring their pursuits—those things that God has placed in their hearts and has given them the ability and desire to do for Him and for others—to Jesus together and ask God to make something of them.

Fulfilling any mighty call of God cannot be done without God's supernatural provision. We can stand strong together and keep going, despite what the world may say. Small groups of people who come together in prayer for the kingdom of God can accomplish great things for God (as seen in chapter 5 of this book).

Small-Group Reflections

1. What are some changes, if any, that you would make to your small-group meetings? How would you explain the rationale for those changes?
2. What are some actions you may need to incorporate in order to receive prayer requests from others that are deep, personal, and important (compared to shallow, impersonal requests)?

Conclusion

5The purpose of my instruction is that all believers would be filled with love that comes from a pure heart, a clear conscience, and genuine faith. 6But some people have missed this whole point. They have turned away from these things and spend their time in meaningless discussions.

1 Timothy 1:5-6

Many so-called Christians fail to fulfill their calling because they get into a religious cycle of observing rituals and feel that they have already accomplished God's calling for them. The truth is that God often has a world-changing calling for each believer, a calling to influence many for the Lord (Matthew 5:16; John 13:15; 1 Timothy 4:12; 1 Peter 2:12, 21), and this might not just be limited to doing well in our careers and running our businesses.

Fulfilling one's calling has to do with the heart, which is for the Lord, and therefore is for others. It has to do with our dependence on God and our trust in the Lord to make paths for us. By our own strength, there is not much we can do, but by the power of the Holy Spirit, there is nothing that we cannot do.

So how can we grow in our heart for the Lord, especially as Ephesians 4 directs us? We need to be disciples of Jesus. We need to be honest with ourselves, we need to see how we are in relationship with God and others, and we need to realize where God is leading us.

In discipleship, we will share lives together. We will be open to others who will scrutinize the state of our soul and spirit. Others who have the Spirit of God may also give us guidance and direction. God will lead us together and individually through our small groups.

Small groups are a way that Jesus developed His disciples, who in turn made more disciples. A small group is a way for relationships to deepen, which translates to deeper relationships with God. Small groups have been shown to be an effective way for Christians to welcome not-yet-believers into their midst. There may certainly be times for congregational worship, Bible studies, and accomplishing organizational missions, but small groups that are focused on life-on-life sharing will make Christians into disciples of Jesus who are able to make other disciples.

It is through small groups that discipleship can be restored in the Church. Discipleship involves sharing lives over time, and that leads to Christians fulfilling their highest calling, which is love, or God Himself.

So, brothers and sisters, our return to the Lord is a return to each other. The love that we have for one another will prove to the world that we are Jesus's disciples. It is through that love that many will come to encounter and experience God.

Though each of us may have different callings to fulfill, our highest and unified calling is to love. Without love, even our greatest accomplishments for the kingdom of God may be counted as nothing (1 Corinthians 13:1–3). Love is the most difficult pursuit, and many will settle for less. However, let us not shrink back, but let us keep on going to the full and complete standard of Christ. Let us love one another and fulfill the call of the Great Commandment, which leads to the Great Commission. May we make disciples of Jesus while going, baptizing, and teaching, as we grow in discipleship ourselves.

Today, many nations know Christ as a result of small groups that have gathered to seek God together. They sought God in prayer and acted together as God led them.

There is more to come, and the calling rests with you, brothers and sisters of Christ—you who grow personally and collectively through discipleship in small groups.

> *Dear friends, let us continue to love one another, for love comes from God. Anyone who loves is a child of God and knows God. But anyone who does not love does not know God, for God is love.*
>
> 1 John 4:7–8

> *He makes the whole body fit together perfectly. As each part does its own special work, it helps the other parts grow, so that the whole body is healthy and growing and full of love.*
>
> Ephesians 4:16

> *7For God has not given us a spirit of fear and timidity, but of power, love, and self-discipline.*
>
> 2Timothy 1:7

End Notes

Chapter 1. The Great Commission

1. William Mounce, "Εὐαγγελίζω," accessed March 23, 2020, https://www.billmounce.com/greek-dictionary/euangelizo.

2. Vladimir Ubeivolc, *Rethinking Missio Dei among Evangelical Churches in an Eastern European Orthodox Context* (Carlisle, Cumbria, UK: Langham Monographs, 2016), 7.

3. Gerhard Kittel, Gerhard Friedrich, and Geoffrey W. Bromiley, eds., *Theological Dictionary of the New Testament: Abridged in One Volume* (Grand Rapids: Eerdmans, 1985), 632–635.

4. J. D. Douglas and Merrill C. Tenney, *Zondervan's Pictorial Bible Dictionary* (Grand Rapids: Zondervan Academic, 1999), 273.

5. "40. Hagios," Bible Hub, accessed May 15, 2019, http://biblehub.com/greek/40.htm.

6. "1484. Ἔθνη (Ethnē)," Bible Hub, accessed May 15, 2019, http://biblehub.com/greek/ethne__1484.htm.

7. William Mounce, "Great Commission and Participles," accessed September 21, 2019, https://billmounce.com/monday-with-mounce/great-commission-and-participles.

8. William Mounce, "Lecture on the Orientation," accessed September 22, 2019, https://www.billmounce.com/biblestudygreek/orientation/lecture.

9. "4198. Πορεύομαι (Poreuomai)," Bible Hub, accessed May 15, 2019, http://biblehub.com/greek/4198.htm.

10. "1321. Διδάσκω (Didaskó)," Bible Hub, accessed May 15, 2019, http://biblehub.com/greek/1321.htm.

11. Nabeel Qureshi, *Seeking Allah, Finding Jesus: A Devout Muslim Encounters Christianity* (Grand Rapids: Zondervan, 2016).

12. "907. Βαπτίζω (Baptizó)," Bible Hub, accessed May 15, 2019, http://biblehub.com/greek/907.htm.

13. "What Is Baptism?" Hillsong, accessed May 15, 2019, https://hillsong.com/faith/baptism/.

14. William Mounce, "Τηρέω," accessed May 15, 2019, https://www.billmounce.com/greek-dictionary/tereo.

15. "3326. Μετά (Meta)," Bible Hub, accessed May 15, 2019, http://biblehub.com/greek/3326.htm.

16. "Bystander Effect," Wikipedia, accessed January 30, 2019, https://en.wikipedia.org/wiki/Bystander_effect.

Chapter 2. The Good News Explained

17. Samuel S. Goebel (Presented at the Morning Reflections, Charlotte, North Carolina, July 24, 2019).

18. For more details on the process that is involved before a person is saved, see: Sang Kwan Lee, *The Gospel that Jesus Taught: The Gospel of the Kingdom* (Seoul Korea, 2010).

19. An example of the Sinner's Prayer from "Four Spiritual Laws" from CRU (formerly known as Campus Crusade for Christ): "Lord Jesus, I need You. Thank You for dying on the cross for my sins. I open the door of my life and receive You as my Savior and Lord. Thank You for forgiving my sins and giving me eternal life. Take control of the throne of my life. Make me the kind of person You want me to be."

20. John Wesley, *Journal of John Wesley*, Christian Classics Ethereal Library, accessed September 21, 2017, https://www.ccel.org/ccel/wesley/journal.vi.ii.xvi.html.

21. "Strangely Warmed," *Good News*, accessed September 13, 2017, https://goodnewsmag.org/2017/07/strangely-warmed/.

22. "Why Do People Brag About Being Busy?" *Huffington Post*, October 28, 2016, http://www.huffingtonpost.com/quora/why-do-people-brag-about_b_12692178.html.

23. "The End of Solitude: In a Hyperconnected World, Are We Losing the Art of Being Alone?" NewStatesman, http://www.newstatesman.com/2017/04/end-solitude-hyperconnected-world-are-we-losing-art-being-alone.

24. Sam Hwang (Presented at the Ambassadors Conference 2017, Central Presbyterian Church, Little Neck, NY, May 28, 2017), https://www.ambassadorsconference.org/.

25. This question is similar to that of the rich young man who asked Jesus what "good" he must do to earn eternal life in Matthew 19:16. Jesus pointed him to God, who is the only One able to provide eternal life, not some good works initiated by an individual. Jesus was telling the rich young man that he must keep the First and Second Commandments, which are to love God with all his heart, mind, and soul (Matthew 22:37–38) and to love others as yourself (Matthew 22:39), but he misunderstood it to mean that he would be considered perfect by "doing" those things. That is why Jesus told this rich young man to remove what was distancing him from God and others, which

were his riches. The relationship is what mattered. The relationship with others demonstrates the believer's growing relationship with God, which is how a person is given perfected faith, or eternal life.

26. "What Is the Gospel?" Prayer Tents, accessed September 22, 2017, https://www.prayertents.com/gospel101.

Chapter 3. How Jesus and His Disciples Made Other Disciples

27. Unknown.

28. See Matthew 9:9–13. This shows how Matthew was called to be Jesus's disciple. When the Pharisees asked why Jesus associated with sinners like tax collectors, Jesus responded that He was after those *who know they are sinners*. In other words, they recognize that there is some void in them and recognize a need for God.

29. This is why Prayer Tents was formed. Prayer Tents provides a way for Christians to be available at those times when people find an interest in God within close proximity so that the discipleship can begin. Find out more at https://www.prayertents.com/aboutus.

30. Acts 2:42: *All the believers devoted themselves to the apostles' teaching.*

Chapter 4. History of the Gospel, Evangelism, and Missions

31. Acts 6:1 talks about possible issues that will arise when unique small groups exist. Note that the Church did not remove these small groups because of them, but rather they put administrators over them, specifically people who are filled with the Holy Spirit.

32. Julianne Cox, Speech, "Ephesians 2," October 5, 2017.

33. James B. Twitchell, *Shopping for God: How Christianity Went from in Your Heart to in Your Face* (New York: Simon & Schuster, 2007), 20. Twitchell refers to this quote because it is "so on point." This quote is traditionally attributed to Richard Halverson, former chaplain of the United States Senate; however, similar quotes have been circulated in the past.

34. "First Council of Nicaea," *Catholic Encyclopedia*, New Advent, accessed December 6, 2017, http://www.newadvent.org/cathen/11044a.htm.

35. Cyrille Vogel, *Le Pécheur et la pénitence dans l'Église ancienne* (Paris: Cerf, 1982), 14–15. This also matches the description provided in Acts, especially in Acts 2:42–47.

36. Jack Zavada, "Asceticism," Learn Religions, accessed July 3, 2020, https://www.learnreligions.com/what-is-asceticism-700046.

37. Vogel, *Le Pécheur*, 36.

38. Charles-Louis Richard and Jean Joseph Giraud, *Bibliothèque sacrée* (Paris: Méquignon Fils Ainé, 1822), http://archive.org/details/bibliothquesac01rich.

39. Oliver Davies and Thomas O'Loughlin, eds., *Celtic Spirituality* (New York: Paulist Press, 2000), 49–50.

40. Robert L. Fastiggi, *The Sacrament of Reconciliation: An Anthropological and Scriptural Understanding* (Chicago: Hillenbrand Books, 2017), 102.

41. Kate Dooley, "From Penance to Confession: The Celtic Contribution," *Bijdragen* 43, no. 4 (January 1, 1982): 390–411, https://doi.org/10.1080/00062278.1982.10554351.

42. Enrico dal Covolo, "The Historical Origin of Indulgences," Catholic Culture, http://www.catholicculture.org/culture/library/view.cfm?recnum=1054.

43. "Purgatory: The Purifying Fire," Catholic News Agency, accessed December 12, 2017, https://www.catholicnewsagency.com/resources/apologetics/purgatory/purgatory-the-purifying-fire.

44. "Confession," CatholiCity, accessed December 12, 2017, https://www.catholicity.com/baltimore-catechism/lesson31.html.

45. Aron Moss, "Do Jews Believe in Hell?" Chabad.org, accessed December 12, 2017, http://www.chabad.org/library/article_cdo/aid/1594422/jewish/Do-Jews-Believe-in-Hell.htm.

46. "Catechism of the Catholic Church," The Holy See, accessed December 12, 2017, http://www.vatican.va/archive/ENG0015/__P4G.HTM.

47. "The Reformation," *Catholic Encyclopedia*, New Advent, accessed December 12, 2017, http://www.newadvent.org/cathen/12700b.htm.

48. "Library: The Historical Origin of Indulgences," CatholicCulture.org, accessed July 5, 2020, https://www.catholicculture.org/culture/library/view.cfm?recnum=1054.

49. Randy Petersen, "Selling Forgiveness: How Money Sparked the Protestant Reformation," Christianity Today, accessed December 12, 2017, http://www.christianitytoday.com/history/issues/issue-14/selling-forgiveness-how-money-sparked-protestant.html.

50. "Library," CatholicCulture.org.

51. "Indulgence Explained," Everything.Explained.Today, accessed July 5, 2020, http://everything.explained.today/Indulgence/.

52. Alexis Soyer, *The Pantropheon: Or a History of Food and Its Preparation in Ancient Times* (New York: Paddington Press, 1977), 172.

53. "Reformation," *Encyclopedia Britannica*, accessed December 13, 2017, https://www.britannica.com/event/Reformation.

54. Justin Holcomb, "The Five Solas—Points from the Past That Should Matter to You," Christianity.com, accessed December 13, 2017, https://www.christianity.com/church/church-history/the-five-solas-of-the-protestant-reformation.html.

55. Note that the word *catholic* means "universal," meaning they are unified and have one teaching.

56. "The Crusades: Indulgences and Penance," Erenow, accessed December 19, 2017, https://erenow.com/postclassical/crusades/477.html.

57. "Martin Luther and the 95 Theses," History.com, accessed December 7, 2017, http://www.history.com/topics/martin-luther-and-the-95-theses.

58. Henry Zecher, "The Bible Translation That Rocked the World," Christianity Today, accessed December 7, 2017, http://www.christianitytoday.com/history/issues/issue-34/bible-translation-that-rocked-world.html.

59. "Did the Catholic Church Forbid Bible Reading?" CatholicBridge.com, accessed December 7, 2017, http://catholicbridge.com/catholic/did_the_catholic_church_forbid_bible_reading.php.

60. Rusty Roberson, "Enlightened Piety during the Age of Benevolence: The Christian Knowledge Movement in the British Atlantic World," *Church History* 85, no. 2 (June 2016): 246–274.

61. Annette G. Aubert, *The German Roots of Nineteenth-Century American Theology* (Oxford: Oxford University Press, 2013), 119.

62. Timothy J. Keller, *The Reason for God: Belief in an Age of Skepticism* (New York: Penguin Press, 2008), 85.

63. Kevin M. Watson, *The Class Meeting: Reclaiming a Forgotten (and Essential) Small Group Experience* (Wilmore, KY: Seedbed Publishing, 2013), 215–220, Kindle.

64. Brandon O'Brien, "Is Ministry a Job or Vocation?" Christianity Today, accessed December 7, 2017, http://www.christianitytoday.com/pastors/2010/july-online-only/is-ministry-job-or-vocation.html.

65. "Assembly Line," BusinessDictionary.com, accessed December 6, 2017, http://www.businessdictionary.com/definition/assembly-line.html.

66. "Church Pastor: Job Description and Career Requirements," Study.com, accessed December 7, 2017,

http://study.com/articles/Church_Pastor_Job_Information_and_Requirements_for_Students_Considering_a_Career_as_a_Church_Pastor.html.

67. "Average Pastor Salary," PayScale, accessed December 7, 2017, \https://www.payscale.com/research/US/Job=Pastor/Salary.

68. Carey Nieuwhof, "Is Church Online a Front Door—Or a Back Door—for Your Church?" CareyNieuwhof.Com, accessed December 7, 2017, https://careynieuwhof.com/is-church-online-a-front-door-or-a-back-door-for-your-church/.

69. Watson, *The Class Meeting*, 477–478.

70. Watson, *The Class Meeting*, 822–824.

71. Leslie K. Tarr, "John Wesley," Christianity Today, accessed December 6, 2017, http://www.christianitytoday.com/history/people/denominationalfounders/john-wesley.html.

72. Wesley, Journal.

73. Wesley had already called himself a Christian prior to this. In fact, he was a "pastor" when he came to faith in God.

74. Watson, *The Class Meeting*, 351–353.

75. Tarr, "John Wesley."

76. Kevin M. Watson, "John Wesley's Thoughts Upon Methodism (Part IV)" accessed December 6, 2017, https://vitalpiety.com/2007/07/16/john-wesleys-thoughts-upon-methodism-part-iv/.

77. Watson, *The Class Meeting*, 277–281.

78. Watson, *The Class Meeting*, 377.

79. Watson, *The Class Meeting*, 410–413.

80. Watson, *The Class Meeting*, 227–241.

81. Watson, *The Class Meeting*, 183–189.

82. Watson, *The Class Meeting*, 413–420.

83. Watson, *The Class Meeting*, 425–435.

84. Watson, *The Class Meeting*, 454–459.

85. Watson, *The Class Meeting*, 741–747.

86. Watson, *The Class Meeting*, 277–281.

87. Watson, *The Class Meeting*, 802–808.

88. Watson, *The Class Meeting*, 831–832.

89. Watson, *The Class Meeting*, 839–840.

90. Watson, *The Class Meeting*, 841–842.

Chapter 5. Effective Strategies for Evangelism

91. Ralph D. Winter and Steven C. Hawthorne, eds., *Perspectives on the World Christian Movement: A Reader* (Pasadena: William Carey Library, 2013), 34.

92. Paul Pierson, *The Dynamics of Christian Mission: History through a Missiological Perspective* (Pasadena: William Carey International University Press, 2009), 180.

93. Pierson, *Dynamics*, 183.

94. Pierson, *Dynamics*, 188.

95. Ralph D. Winter, *The 25 Unbelievable Years 1945–1969* (Pasadena: William Carey Library, 1969), 78.

96. Winter, *Unbelievable Years*, 78.

97. Zinzendorf was from a family of nobility. He was able to take the Moravians in because he lived in a large house. This shows that God can use the wealthy for His purposes. Operating a business for God, being a tentmaker, will be covered in later sections.

98. Pierson, *Dynamics*, 190.

99. Winter, *Unbelievable Years*, 79.

100. Pierson, *Dynamics*, 194.

101. Pierson, *Dynamics*, 195.

102. *Missio Dei* means "the mission of or sending of God." This may generally be recognized as the Great Commission of Jesus, but it actually goes back to Genesis 12, where God sends Abraham to be a blessing to all nations (Genesis 12:2–3).

103. Pierson, *Dynamics*, 203.

104. Pierson, *Dynamics*, 203.

105. Ralph D. Winter, "The Two Structures of God's Redemptive Mission," *Practical Anthropology* 2, no. 1 (January 1, 1974): 126.

106. Pierson, *Dynamic*, 6.

107. CBMC has expanded beyond its origin in the United States. There is also CBMC International and other regional groups such as the Korean KCBMC.

The International and Korean groups welcome women for historical purposes, and so they had to undergo acronym changes that differ from the original CBMC USA. This is why when one looks up CBMC, one may find the acronym spelled out as "Christian Business & Marketplace Connection" or "Connecting Business and Marketplace to Christ." However, these organizations are united and they welcome and support members from each other. They are all missional organizations that desire to make Jesus known in the marketplace.

108. "The World's Largest Churches," Leadership Network, accessed March 22, 2018, http://leadnet.org/world/.

109. Jin-Woo Lee, *The Influence of Shamanism on Korean Churches and How to Overcome It* (Lynchburg, VA: Liberty Baptist Theological Seminary, 2000), 46, https://digitalcommons.liberty.edu/cgi/viewcontent.cgi?article=1181&context=doctoral.

110. George G. Hunter, *The Celtic Way of Evangelism: How Christianity Can Reach the West . . . Again*, 10th anniversary edition (Nashville: Abingdon Press, 2010), 13–25.

111. Hunter, *Celtic Way*, 56–75.

112. Hunter, *Celtic Way*, 56–75.

113. Winter, *Perspectives*, 241–252.

114. Winter, *Perspectives*, 241–252.

115. Winter, *Perspectives*, 241–252.

116. Patrick Lai, *Tentmaking: The Life and Work of Business as Missions* (Downers Grove, IL: IVP Books, 2006), 331–363.

117. Lai, *Tentmaking*, 361.

118. Stephen Bailey, "Is Business as Mission Honest?" (Spring 2006): 16, https://missionexus.org/is-business-as-mission-honest/.

119. Bailey, "Business as Mission."

120. Bailey, "Business as Mission."

121. Stanley J. Grenz and Roger E. Olson, *Who Needs Theology?: An Invitation to the Study of God* (Downers Grove, IL: InterVarsity Press, 1996), 15.

122. Grenz, *Who Needs Theology?*, 69.

123. Grenz, *Who Needs Theology?*, 68.

124. Grenz, *Who Needs Theology?*, 77.

125. Grenz, *Who Needs Theology?*, 101.

126. Grenz, *Who Needs Theology?*, 95.

127. Grenz, *Who Needs Theology?*, 68–102.

128. Grenz, *Who Needs Theology?*, 108.

129. Grenz, *Who Needs Theology?*, 110–111.

130. Robert J. Schreiter, *Constructing Local Theologies*, 30th anniversary edition (Maryknoll, NY: Orbis Books, 2015), 22–38.

131. Stephen B. Bevans, *Models of Contextual Theology* (Maryknoll, NY: Orbis Books, 2002), 1–15.

132. Schreiter, *Constructing Local Theologies*, 1–21.

133. Schreiter, *Constructing Local Theologies*, 1–21.

134. Dean Flemming, *Contextualization in the New Testament: Patterns for Theology and Mission* (Downers Grove, IL: IVP Academic Press, 2009), 25–55.

135. Bevans, *Models of Contextual Theology*, 15.

136. Bevans, *Models of Contextual Theology*, 54.

137. Bevans, *Models of Contextual Theology*, 59.

138. Bevans, *Models of Contextual Theology*, 103–116.

139. Bevans, *Models of Contextual Theology*, 87.

140. Bevans, *Models of Contextual Theology*, 88–102.

141. Bevans, *Models of Contextual Theology*, 37–53.

142. Bevans, *Models of Contextual Theology*, 117–137.

143. Bevans, *Models of Contextual Theology*, 15.

144. Matthew Cook, Rob Haskell, Ruth Julian, and Natee Tanchanpongs, eds., *Local Theology for the Global Church: Principles for an Evangelical Approach to Contextualization* (Pasadena: William Carey Library, 2010), 125.

145. Ruth A. Tucker, *From Jerusalem to Irian Jaya: A Biographical History of Christian Missions* (Grand Rapids: Zondervan, 2004), 364–398.

146. Tucker, *From Jerusalem*, 364–398.

147. Florence Huntington Jensen, "William Carey," Wholesome Words, accessed March 26, 2018, https://www.wholesomewords.org/missions/bcarey6.html.

148. Paul A. Pomerville, *The Third Force in Missions: A Pentecostal Contribution to Comtemporary Mission Theology* (Peabody, MA: Hendrickson Publishers, 2016), 79–104.

149. Timothy Tennent, *Invitation to World Missions: A Trinitarian Missiology for the Twenty-First Century* (Grand Rapids: Kregel Academic, 2010), 409–431.

150. Pierson, *Dynamics*, 326.

151. Pierson, *Dynamics*, 234.

152. Pierson, *Dynamics*, 320.

Chapter 6. Our Highest Calling is Love

153. Matthew 22:37–40

154. These are the people whom Prayer Tents calls the "Interested." The "Interested" people are temporarily drawn by God to seek Him. For more details, refer to the following webpage: https://www.prayertents.com/interested.

155. *The Secret*, directed by Drew Heriot, 2006.

156. Note that this is an agile term in software development used in the corporate world. What sells in business is the ability to accomplish more in less time with fewer resources. Relationships are not that way. If the corporate world teaches efficiency, the Church must teach patience, especially as it relates to love.

157. *Holy* means to be set apart. This can be seen in various places in Scripture, such as in Exodus 16:23, where the Sabbath is to be a day that is set apart (or different, distinguished) from the rest of the days. Additionally, קֹדֶשׁ (*qodesh*) means "apartness, sacredness, or separateness" (see Strongs #6944).

158. The definition of *busyness* also recognizes that skipping time with others may result in producing more.

159. The Project Management Institute, a global nonprofit professional organization for project management, defines a project to be a temporary endeavor, which means that it has a definite beginning and an end. Love being patient does not define an end.

160. "5541. Χρηστεύομαι (Chrésteuomai), Bible Hub, accessed June 15, 2020, https://biblehub.com/greek/5541.htm.

161. Dr. Sang Sur often delineates the three callings of king, priest, and prophet. He intends to put his teachings in writing in the near future.

162. Min Chung, "The Flesh and the Spirit," accessed June 15, 2020, https://cfchome.org/wp-content/uploads/20161002-The-Flesh-and-The-Spirit.pdf.

163. Healing and restoration from trafficking and other abusive sin is a topic that is big enough to fill many books. Organizations that seek to help people

affected by these sins are seeking people who are able to love. Contact Prayer Tents, and we can help you connect with such organizations.

Chapter 7. Being a Disciple to Make Disciples

164. Sang W. Sur, "Address to Graduate Seminary Students" (Ridgefield, NJ, October 28, 2019).

165. John Wimber and Kevin Springer, *Power Evangelism* (Grand Rapids: Chosen Books, 2009).

166. *Evangelism* is actually the word meaning "to preach or share the gospel." In Ephesians 4:11, it appears as a gift that is given to certain people, not to all Christians. There are two other passages (Mark 16:15 and Matthew 10:7) where Jesus tells His disciples to proclaim the Good News (both verses hint to showing signs and wonders). Evangelism (or preaching/proclaiming/sharing) itself *does not make disciples* of people, but rather is solely an initiator to potentially make disciples.

Dr. Sang Sur is the founder of Prayer Tents, a Christian mission organization that seeks to enable people to find life by meeting Jesus through relationships with Christians near them. He is called to bi-vocational ministry, being a tentmaker as he works with other business leaders to bring many to Christ, while also giving support to the global Church.

Sang is the chief executive officer of Sciturus Real Investment Group, along with its sister companies Hanmaum Realty and Techellence. He is an engineering and business executive who led technology M&A that resulted in $53 million in revenue growth of two major global-reaching companies within the first year. He also directed personnel across all functions of engineering in modernizing aeronautical radar and countermeasure systems that continue to prevent US C-130s and B-52s from being shot down in hostile territories. As an Air Force officer, he was part of the Air Force Special Operations Command, ensuring the best aerial equipment for the US military, particularly the Special Forces. He holds a Ph.D. in Business Administration and Management and two doctorates in fields of ministry (Th.D. and D.Min.).

Sang is also an ordained Christian pastor and a Certified Executive Coach, and he works with Christian executives in the marketplace and with pastors to enable them to go beyond their perceived limits and fulfill their great callings from God. Sang is a member of the Christian Business Men's Connection (CBMC) and chairs the NYC group.

Sang lives in New Jersey with his wife, son, and daughter.

Find out more about him at www.sangsur.com.

Visit us at

ourhighestcalling.com

Share your favorite quotes or ask questions. Explore with other fellow readers, Prayer Tents staff, and the author.

Let's support the Church together in developing relationship-centered small groups that welcome others to discipleship.

www.ingramcontent.com/pod-product-compliance
Lightning Source LLC
Chambersburg PA
CBHW071235070526
44583CB00017B/2199